Crying for a Vision and Other Essays

The Collected Steve Scott
Vol. One

by
Steve Scott

Bloomington, IN Milton Keynes, UK
authorHOUSE

AuthorHouse™
1663 Liberty Drive, Suite 200
Bloomington, IN 47403
www.authorhouse.com
Phone: 1-800-839-8640

AuthorHouse™ UK Ltd.
500 Avebury Boulevard
Central Milton Keynes, MK9 2BE
www.authorhouse.co.uk
Phone: 08001974150

First published by AuthorHouse 2/20/2007

ISBN: 978-1-4259-7744-3 (e)
ISBN: 978-1-4259-7754-2 (sc)

Library of Congress Control Number: 2006910282

Printed in the United States of America
Bloomington, Indiana

This book is printed on acid-free paper.

Cover art by Michael Redmond

Thanks to "GI-rine" Ron Bowles, Tim "Flyboy" Fitch and Jake "the Snake" Geib-Rosch at AuthorHouse.

For more information, please visit our official websites at www.canagroup.org and www.alivingdog.com

Crying for a Vision and Other Essays: The Collected Steve Scott Vol. One

Introduction: A Horse of a Hundred Colors

I once heard a story about two Rabbis arguing about an Old Testament prophecy concerning the Messiah's entry into Jerusalem. One was arguing that a donkey was too lowly a creature to be carrying the Messiah. The second Rabbi replied by asking what kind of creature might be appropriate for such an important task...going on to ask, rhetorically, if a horse of a hundred colors would be sufficient.

The earlier arguments about what art is 'good for' have faded somewhat. They have given way to a number of new questions about Art and the arts in the church. Some of the questions are reminiscent of the story above. What approach to the arts is most appropriate for expressing Christian value? Do we use our expressive skills to uncover the hidden beauty and radiance of an 'ordinary' down to earth world...or do we shape and bend our language 'til it points to a transcendent, luminous alternative?

How we imagine the church and its relation to the Kingdom usually has some bearing on the place we give to the arts. Some of us are cognizant of how arts and media have now soaked into the fabric of every day life, and are looking therefore for media rich ways of engaging the marketplace in order to express and communicate Christian value. Others value the arts above and beyond the mere pragmatics of communication. Art, they suggest, has its own place in a social and cultural order that unfolds under the present/ future reign of God.

However we think about art, we admit that the question gets a bit more complex in this new century. We now live in a world that strikes an uneasy balance between global connectedness and cultural diversity. Each community in the global family brings different traditions, worldview, values and questions woven into its forms of cultural expression.

Some of us have wrestled with the arts in order to make our faith relevant to our context and audience. Others have drawn upon those Biblical passages that speak of worship and God honoring cultural expressions from every tribe and nation, and have gone beyond contextualized bridge building towards an understanding of the coming Kingdom (and its first fruits now) that includes redemption and restoration of many different cultures. Still others have suggested that God's providential common grace lights up all good art, whether it is spiritually motivated or not.

If this were a painted surface, then all three of those 'colors' (and perhaps at least 97 more!) would make their contribution, harmonizing form and content, ground and figure in an overall composition. If this were a piece of music then each thread of melody would unfold, sometimes to be a dominant theme, other times to be harmonically supportive of the other threads. I suspect that we could move through a variety of art forms in search of the metaphoric and symbolic ways in which each one would appropriately honor the diversity of the above approaches and the unity of the overall artwork.

Material/ Sources/ Acknowledgements

The material in this book comes from different sources. *Crying for a Vision* was originally published in book form by Stride books UK in 1991, edited by Rupert Loydell. Stride books, incidentally, is a well-respected alternative small press in the UK, publishing a wide range of material from contemporary art theory, to modern/ postmodern poetry and prose. Please check them out online at www.Stridebooks.co.uk

The essay on Japanese novelist Shusaku Endo was published in *Radix* magazine in 1985, and reprinted in UK's *Third Way* in the early 1990s. The 'Crossing the Boundaries' piece was published in the late '90s by *Radix* (and in an online version by Salon Duarte) and began life as a descriptive lecture that unpacked some of the rationale and the working methods behind the mixed media collaboration 'Crossing the Boundaries' undertaken with painter Gaylen Stewart. That talk, in different forms, has been given in the Philippines, the People's republic of China, Croatia, the Netherlands, and at arts events, festivals and colleges in different parts of the US.

'The Light by which we see' appeared in *Radix* at the beginning of 2001.

Radix magazine, incidentally, has been publishing for more than thirty years and is widely regarded as one of the more thought-provoking, intelligent, engaged and relevant publications with a Faith perspective out there. Check them online. www.radixmagazine.com

'Fear and Multicultural Trembling' was printed in *CIVA Seen*, the multicultural issue in 2003. This publication is produced by CIVA, Christians In the Visual Arts. This organization, with its biannual conferences, summer workshop, traveling shows and regular publications has done a tremendous amount (since the late 1970s) to organize, inform, network and empower art makers who are of the Christian Faith. You can learn more about them here: http: www.civa.org/

'Emotional Tourist' is from an interview conducted with Gord Wilson in 2005, © Gord Wilson, and used by permission (see "Poetry in the UK" at alivingdog.com). The 'Crying for a Vision Study Guide' is © Gord Wilson and used by permission. Some CDs surface from time to time at Radrockers.com. Many thanks, therefore, to all the places where this material first surfaced.

And Finally:

In 1997, Cornerstone Press published my book on the arts, *Like a House on Fire*. This was not, as some suggested, a reference to some kind of apocalyptic melt down of Western Civilization in the flames of Post-Modernism. Five minutes with any online (or print) dictionary that covers UK colloquialisms will tell you the phrase alludes to people getting on well together (they got on like a house on fire!) All the material in this book in your hands either leads up to the *Fire* material, flows around it, or builds upon the ideas sketched in that book. This book and *Like a House on Fire* complement each other, and read together, provide a fair picture of my ideas and opinions. Thanks to Wipf and Stock, publishers, for bringing *Like a House on Fire* back into print. –Steve Scott, Sacramento, CA 2006.

PART ONE:
Crying for a Vision

1. Are You Responsible for This Monstrosity?

Lewis Hyde, in his book 'The Gift'[1] approaches a study of the gift of artistic creativity by describing the complex social and spiritual functions of gift giving and receiving in traditional societies. He argues that such communities were sustained through the complex bindings of obligation and counter-obligation that were woven through the medium of ceremonial gift exchange.

Hyde goes on to talk about our own communities in the developed world and how the developments and shifts in economic theory and practice laid the groundwork for the evolution of the capitalist system. Hyde contrasts the individual in a society like ours who is 'free' to purchase a 'commodity' with 'no strings attached' with the individual who is a member of a traditional gift-giving 'gifting' community, who is thus emotionally, socially and spiritually bonded to that community and its world view.

Hyde proceeds to explore the 'place' of a 'gifted artistic individual' in a culture like ours where perhaps we make the mistake of confusing 'freedom' with autonomy, and 'value' with price. Surely some of the current controversies surrounding the public funding of the arts are rooted and grounded in the above mentioned categories of confusion.

On one hand, we have artists who seem to want to be absolutely free to depict whatever they like at the taxpayer's expense. On the other hand, we have those people that do not seem to recognize the value of the arts to the cultural life of a community. They simply want artistic taste to be dictated by what price an idea, or a particular piece of work can command on the open market, or what kind of support an artist can get by appeals to the private sector. Neither the freedom to make art, nor the artwork itself is recognized as a gift. If it were then perhaps some of the liabilities and responsibilities of gift giving and receiving would be more clearly recognized.

There is a famous Picasso painting called 'Guernica'. This painting is a very expressionistic rendering of the horrific bombing of a small village. Picasso worked in almost monochrome, using blacks, whites, grays, and some pink and red. The images were exaggerated and distorted, but not to the point of abstraction. Apparently, as the story goes, Picasso was standing in front of this painting when a Nazi German officer came up to him. It had been Fascist planes under Franco who had bombed the village. The Nazis had no love of 'decadent' art, art that was not full of the golden glow of traditional values, or supportive of the ideas of the Third Reich. The officer looked at Picasso's painting, full of its horrific imagery, and said to Picasso, *'Are you responsible for this monstrosity?'* (or words to that effect.)

'No,' Picasso replied, *'You are.'*

As we look at some of the questions being raised today around the public funding of controversial art, one of the things that gets overlooked is 'Why is this happening? Why is work like this being offered for public viewing? Who decides that this is viable as art?' Also, I think it is fair to ask, 'Where are the Christians?'

In my opinion, some of us have spent too long on the sidelines, either doing nothing, or offering glib and-ill targeted criticism. In some ways we stand in danger of becoming 'responsible by omission' for whatever fills the cultural void in the name of modern art. Those of us who have ventured out and attempted something in the arts have sometimes had our work and theory hampered by the wrong kind of thinking about what was possible or permissible in the name of a Christian approach to the arts.

Reading Hyde's book opened my eyes in a new way to the delicate relationship between grace and works. We, as Christians, are sacrificially responsive to God, in the light of the wonderful grace gift of His only Son. While Christians are united in their appreciation of the precious gift of God's son, and are committed at least in theory to the idea of diversity in the church, they tend to go in different directions when it comes to the arts.

Some are still suspicious of the arts, fearing too close an attachment to 'the things of the world.' Others believe that the arts have some value in communicating Christian truth across cultures. They believe that the shared common heritage of storytelling, singing and picture making may open doors for communication where other approaches might not succeed. Still others see the arts as integral to worship within the body of Christ, while some see their attempt doing 'the good work' as sufficiently glorifying to God, with no need for overtly spiritual agendas to justify their artmaking.

I personally believe that the arts are important for the church for at least three reasons.

Firstly, both practice and enjoyment of the arts demonstrate and celebrate the creative aspects of our redeemed humanity.

Secondly, creative artmaking is a bridge of communication across cultures.[2]

Thirdly, the arts provide more dynamic models for theological discussion. These ideas, plus some others, are looked at in what follows.

The following materials can be best described as an exploratory overview of some of the issues that I believe are important in thinking through how we as Christians respond to art, either as audience or as creators. I try to look at ways of understanding some aspects of the modem arts in our own culture, while also paying attention to the very different ways the arts are seen and used in other cultures. The materials began life in a variety of ways. Some began as small group Bible studies and later grew into full-blown lectures delivered to artists and students in different educational settings. An early chapter in this book is based upon a magazine article (from which the book's title is taken) published some years ago.[3] Another chapter is a revised version of a lecture given in 1989 at a Christian Arts conference in Bali, Indonesia.

I would stress that all the materials should be regarded as 'in process' rather than as final statements on what is a very large and complex issue. I should also stress that my own thinking on the subjects commented upon in these chapters has been greatly enriched by dialogue with artists, thinkers, students and missionaries from literally all over the world.

2. The Act of Seeing With One's Own Eyes.

Before we can come to grips with the complexities of making art, even 'message' art, we must first consider how to look at art, and learn to understand its many messages to us. The business of looking at art is ultimately going to be one of personal response. In order to inform and undergird our response I want to address four possible ways of thinking about and looking at art that have surfaced in recent art history.

1. Inside Looking Out

This involves an approach to art that focuses simply on the qualities of a given medium (let us say paint on canvas) and its use in terms of color, line, design and balance. This evaluation of an art object purely in terms of its 'formal' or design qualities tries to screen out all other elements from the reading of the work. An artist that works in this way is trying to make an art that is 'true to itself' acutely in terms of relationships established by line, color etc within the framework of the picture. Art like this is set up to be contemplated as being beautiful for 'its own sake.' The artist is often described as highly sensitized and incredibly gifted. Sometimes the artist is hailed as an inspired genius.

This elevation of the artist is not specifically linked to the stripping down and 'purification' of art. I am simply trying to point out the 'family resemblance' between some of these ideas. If the object is seen as pure and self-contained, and its maker hailed as a gifted hero, then the 'true' experience of art, accordingly, must be a pure 'disinterested' form of absorbed contemplation that seeks to capture the 'essence' of the art object on view.

For some artists the quest for the 'purity' of art has led them to try and step outside of the limiting influences of the picture frame and the sculpture plinth. It has even led them to seek a way of escape from the corrupting influence of the gallery system. The art object, and its attendant support structure, largely disappear as the artist moves into performance, concept, process and situation. As we shall see, these points of view are vulnerable to a number of critical perspectives. Is it right to assign such a privileged, almost mystical status to the artmakers and their creativity? Is 'disinterested contemplation' the only, or even the most appropriate response to art? And is art that focuses exclusively inward necessarily 'purer' and more art-like than art that refers outward?

Some writers, such as Suzi Gablik, have suggested that modern art, in seeking its own autonomy, far from becoming purer has merely been neutralized. It has nothing to say to the world, especially our current situation. As art critic and thinker Suzi Gablik points out:

> *In the name of radical autonomy, it is the pure and disinterested artwork which can be most readily harnessed into the social process, which lends itself most easily to co-optation by the economic apparatus.*[4]

2. Down Looking Up

This point of view is rooted and grounded in a 'material' view of culture. Critics writing from this perspective have little trouble with approaches to craft and popular art that make use of a surplus of raw materials, or are partially the result of increasingly sophisticated technology of production. What they take issue with is how ideas about art and the role of the artist have developed in cultures like ours. Such ideas about art and the artist, and some of our current art practices, are regarded with some suspicion. The artwork and the corresponding myth of the 'special, creative artist' are seen as a symptom of the deep alienation produced by our capitalist economic system.

The key assumptions that inform the worldview are seen as less 'unexamined' and more 'consciously maintained' by those with money, power and privilege in order to keep things just as they are. Art and its supporting myth of the unique inspired artist are seen as part of a system of mystification, with art subtly supporting the status quo by what the artist chooses to show and alternatively to leave out of pictures.[5] Art depicts what is beautiful and desirable, and concepts of value are linked to notions of commodity and rarity. It is not that the rich get to buy great art, but rather, what the wealthy own is by definition good.[6]

A similar kind of analysis sees art less in terms of a window onto a culture whose 'alienated consumption' is an outworking of its base economic values, but more in terms of a symptom of a culture as a whole living out the implications of being 'in flight from God.' A post-Christian society that has replaced the true God with gods of its own making will experience the consequences of its choice. These consequences can be traced through many levels including the history of its art. As art moves through its phases of searching for, and then abandoning a quest for universal, corporate, or even personal meaning then there is a corresponding disintegration of form.

Some, like Hans Rookmaker and Francis Schaeffer read an underlying narrative of despair in the art products of a society that has drifted from its Judeo-Christian moorings.[7] Other writers, such as Peter Fuller, link this 'narrative' back to the loss of a shared symbolic order and the absence of a vital esthetic dimension in modern day society.[8]

Writers such as Suzi Gablik and Nicholas Wolterstorff (coming from very different world views) suggest that the collapse of meaning and resulting bankruptcy of content in some forms of modern art can be traced to the divorce between art and the rest of life. The subsequent specialization in the field of the arts parallels similar developments that occurred in philosophical and scientific thinking and practice in the wake of both the Enlightenment, and the Industrial Revolution.[9]

All of these analytical frameworks, from the Marxist one of John Berger through to the 'emerging paradigm' model of Suzi Gablik look both *at* current art, and *through* it onto an underlying social and cultural condition.

Some artists have attempted to build upon some of the various suspicions about art, by creating 'anti-art' that was to be strategically injected into the vacuum that art has left in order to prophetically confront society from the platform of its own culture. Both Dada and punk rock serve as two recent examples of attempts to use artspace and art vocabulary to declare the end of art, puncture the mystique of the artist, and then proceed to some sort of radical social analysis. It did not work.

If art as 'pure object' presented no threat and was readily co-opted, then anti-art was reabsorbed by what Herbert Marcuse describes as a 'repressive tolerance' in which revolutionary and subversive elements are effectively neutralized by assimilation into the dominant social structures where they undergo repackaging as commodities. The revolution is marketed back to the masses. It enters the cycle of 'alienated consumption' by 'selling' the illusion of effective confrontation.

3. Outside Looking In

This approach is similar to the 'down looking up' approach, but rather than seeing art as a window into a world of capitalist 'alienated consumption' or 'post Christian' despair, it approaches art as a system of signs with a supporting context in our particular model of reality or 'world view.' This approach is taken by cultural historians and anthropologists looking into our culture and examining the role the arts play in a society like ours. What role(s) do the arts play in holding up our particular worldview, and what 'non art' factors play into our appreciation and reading of the arts?

In our culture we are used to seeing objects displayed for consideration and contemplation in a museum or a gallery. In some ways, the museum functions as a 'framing device' signaling to us that what enters it is worthy of being looked at a certain way. The museum, itself a relatively recent concept, has had a profound effect on what we are prepared to consider as 'art.[10] Not only where we put objects, but what experts say about them, also plays into how we look at them.

Expert critical responses enter into our field of 'subsidiary awareness' (why was this displayed in the first place? What underlying characteristics or meaning are we meant to be looking for?) and subtly influence the way we look at art from our own culture, and also how we view objects removed from other cultural contexts and put on display in our own. If these conceptual 'framing devices' play a role in how we use art in the sustaining of our world view, then very different devices must operate in those cultures where art is still part of life, and is employed in ritual and ceremony.

Our own accurate understanding of those other worldviews and uses of art have been further undermined in the past by both our esthetic and also our political philosophy. A ritual object 'from the colonies' might start out its museum life as one of the spoils of imperialist expansion, and then be later rehabilitated as an art object displayed for contemplation of its beauty.

In the past some 'primitive' art, viewed through the 'framing device' of the theory of evolution was talked of dismissively and patronizingly as being inferior because it did not meet our criteria in terms of representational accuracy or stylistic design. We would take the criteria for artistic excellence peculiar to our culture, marry them to a hypothesis about how biological and cultural life developed, and pronounce judgment on everything that did not quite measure up to our standards.

For many of us it takes a conscious effort to step back from the limitations of our worldview, and all the unquestioned assumptions and subtle 'conceptual frames' that play a role in supporting it. It is only as we do this that we can take an 'outside looking in' approach, and recognize that among the plurality of cultures, there are many different kinds of art and different reasons for making it.

This approach is necessarily limited because it shifts attention away from individual art objects and towards art as part of a sign system within a given culture. It also raises, but does not fully answer, some very important questions. Is the way in which we experience art purely and simply a product of our cultural history and world view or is there something more? Nicholas Wolterstorff has argued that museum based 'disinterested contemplation' of art is a specific development within our culture in the West.

Peter Fuller, on the other hand, has suggested a 'transcultural' basis for esthetic appreciation grounded in the infant's experience of 'potential space' and fantasy, as it grows in awareness of its identity, separate from the mother. The anthropologist Jacques Maquet, drawing upon his experiences in Theravada Buddhist meditation in Sri Lanka and parts of South East Asia has written of a 'frame of mind' that is shared by different cultures. In our culture it surfaces as absorbed contemplation in the qualities of an art object. In other cultures, it surfaces as an integral part of their life system.[11]

4. Change Consciousness/ Perception

If the pursuit of a cross-cultural equivalent to aesthetic contemplation ends up for some in the meditative traditions that locate ultimate reality in absorption in the thing in and of itself, then it would follow that some artists would look for ways of using their work, or the artistic situation to initiate not so much an aesthetic experience as an overall change of consciousness.

For some, the art object may be the stepping stone into the realization of the oneness of all things. For others the radically 'non-art' nature of their work may be conceived as a visual or sonic equivalent to a riddle or Zen *koan*, designed to explode the limitations of conceptual thought and analysis, and awaken the hearer or viewer to an intense experience of the 'life they are now living.'

Composer John Cage has used random compositional strategies, and even silence, to try and awaken this consciousness in the hearer. Invariably there has been misunderstanding and some complaints.

> *"To all such complaints and criticisms, Cage's answer is basically the same. He believes that the world is changing more rapidly and more drastically than most people realize. A great many of the traditional attitudes of Western thought will soon be obsolete, he feels, and a great many of the older traditions are becoming increasingly relevant to life in the West. Cage insists that the true function of art in our time is to open up the minds and hearts of contemporary men and women to the immensity of these changes, in order that they may be able to 'wake up to the very life' they are living in the modern world."* [12]

Artists have appealed to Eastern meditative traditions, the speculative areas of physics and the 'chaos' theory of science, in order to locate a larger more 'inclusive' sense of order beneath the apparently random surface of their work or 'non' work. They have attempted to purify perception and consciousness by presenting 'pure' objects that have no frame of reference outside of their own immediate presence (steel boxes, etc.) or they have abandoned the notion of object in favor of 'process' and they have planted seeds, grown mold, and documented other forms of organic change.

Again the privileged concept of artist and resolved work comes under critique, but now more from a philosophical point of view rather than a political or an anthropological one. In a recent interview, composer John Cage was asked how he felt twenty years on from the premier of his notorious 'piano' piece 'Silence.' His reply was, 'We have mined the silence.'

Can we, in this very general and provisional overview, determine any overall trends? I would like to suggest at least three.

1). A reading of recent art history reveals an ongoing attempt at purification. At one point there was the 'Formalist' approach to modern art, with work that only referred to arrangements and properties of chosen media. This was about as 'pure' as seemed possible, with no reference outside of 'itself.' Beyond that, artists seemed to move beyond the 'entrapment' of the canvas, frame and sculpture plinth. They tried to step outside the 'gallery' and its 'commodification' of art with its emphasis on material and object. They sought greater purity in idea, performance, process and situation.

2). 'Postmodernism' with its ironic reappropriation of a wide variety of earlier artistic styles, has been argued by some to be an attempt to extend the quest for this 'purity' by exploring and examining the public arena for 'art' and the artist. Artists and thinkers working in this arena often 'quote' from earlier areas of art history in a reflective or an ironic way, allowing the new context to change the 'meaning' of the image or images they have selected. Work like this draws upon art history, while sometimes changing the way we read it.

3). Recent (twentieth century) art history is also full of examples of artists combining different media. The early experiments in collage brought everything from cork, wine bottle labels, tram tickets and photographic images onto the surface of the picture already rendered 'anxious' by explorations into color and theories of perception. The progress from collage to full blown environmental installations is paralleled by the growth in the areas of multimedia performance from the earliest Symbolist, Futurist and Dada events to the work of people like Laurie Anderson today.

We have identified three trends. They are: 1). An ongoing quest for purity; 2). A reflective, 'critical' handling of art traditions and history, and 3). The growth of ideas and work that stretches across and combines many different media. None of the above descriptive categories are exclusive and solitary. There is bound to be some interface and overlap.

Our response as Christians will be to realize that all art has a message. The artist intends a message, or a body of critical thought projects one onto the surface of the object. Sometimes people attempt to 'read between the lines' and extract a message of their own. In all these cases 'message' art is 'art' first. We will see that a slipshod, superficial analysis of culture(s) or a halfhearted dabbling in the media is rooted in the fear or distrust of 'the world.' This attitude has more in common with Greek philosophy, and some eastern religious ideas, than genuinely biblical Christianity.

Maybe we need, as artists, to stretch and play a little to shake off the years of 'spiritual' cobwebs, and break out of the straitjacket of sugar-coated pietism. Maybe we need a more trenchant analysis that attacks accepted models of beauty and truth, and also challenges the mythic status of the artist. Maybe we need to come to terms with a plurality of cultures, all of them judged by Christ. I think we should study hard and learn from the historic 'cloud of witnesses,' made up of those who are Christians, or have explored Christian themes in the art of their time.

For example, Christian poetry has a rich and varied lineage from the fourth century liturgies of Ephraem of Syria to the twentieth century lyrics of Bruce Cockburn. As a tradition Christian poetry is broad enough to encompass the passionate lyrics to Christ of Richard Rolle in thirteenth century England to John of the Cross in sixteenth century counter-Reformation Spain.

It has led to radical experimentation in the relationship between form and content as in the work of seventeenth century poet George Herbert. Poets as diverse as the Puritan Edward Taylor, writing some fifty years after Herbert, to the twentieth century poet David Jones have drawn upon the Eucharist as a source of inspiration, Taylor's meditative 'preparatory journal' is rooted and grounded in his private reflections prior to Communion. Jones's work uses a multileveled exploratory poetic form to 'sacramentally' gather up the fragments of Britain's previous ages and cultures and offer them back to God.

Painters George Rouault and Marc Chagall have invested Biblical themes with personal vision, resulting in novel and startling images. Visser'T Hooft's study of Rembrandt suggests that the changes in his painting and portraiture (especially of Christ) reveal the process of his deepening awareness of and experience in Christian truth.'[13]

The lives and work of many other painters, architects, liturgists, hymnists, composers and dramatists reveal patterns of interaction between a growing faith and a deepening sensibility of creative vocation. Some of these artists worked in ways now being rediscovered and rehabilitated as modernist or post modernist in their feel. Others demonstrated a continuity and community of spirit with those of us seeking to make art in the late twentieth century. Perhaps attention to other Christian artists in diverse times and cultures will help us overcome our sense of rootlessness and isolation. There is nothing new under the sun.'[14]

We also need to do some thinking and creative work that might be sensible to an analysis of cultural plurality and art history from a truly Christian point of view. We will want to do art work that is 'good work' but also moves critically against the unexamined assumptions of the world of art. Christian artists, while wanting to rescue the centrality and dignity of their calling from the ignorance of those who place no value in the arts and mask their fear with 'spiritual' language, will nonetheless see themselves less as a *'Co-Creator'* (the romantic, post-Enlightenment, western ideal) and more as a *Covenant partner* working hand in hand with a sovereignly gracious God.'[15]

We as Christians in the modern art world should embark on our own quest for purity. This is not a call for censorship, nor are we to join the headlong flight towards the void of 'pure' non-reference. We should start critically examining the religious and Christological heresies that infect our understanding of the full import of the Incarnation, and therefore our relationship to the world. Finally, we should briefly go back over the four categories mapped out earlier, to see where we as Christian artists can possibly fit in.

Firstly (or lastly, as I am reversing their order) we thought about the attempt on the part of some, like John Cage to alter our entire conscious relationship to the life that we live. It was Thomas Traherne who said 'you never see the world aright' until you awake to the true status of yourself as a child before God. This renewed 'right seeing' can involve a delight in form, process, order and waking up to the life we are already in.

We, as Christians, will not necessarily see this 'change in consciousness' so much in terms of pure 'objectness' or as waking up to some impersonal order 'beneath' the apparent randomness of life. All processes and our contemplation of them can be seen less as outworking of intrinsic laws, and more in terms of 'covenant' and perhaps even 'narrative.' The Logos has a human stamp in Jesus. 'The mystery of providence' has a distinctly personal touch.

We will also respond to the riches and challenges presented to us by a diversity of cultures, in light of the dynamic lordship of Christ over all cultures. Museum and gallery art has its merit, but we should also wake up to the many uses of art elsewhere in our culture, for example the attempt made by those like William Morris to bring the esthetic dimension into 'everyday life'.

We will remember also the uses of art in assessment of growth and development of children, as well as the therapeutic and humanizing role the arts can play in working with the developmentally disabled. Art becomes part of the vocabulary of the marginalized, giving them dignity and a dynamic symbolic vocabulary.

Also, the arts have dynamic contextual meaning in other cultures as carriers of traditions, or transporters, to other realms. The creative tension between gallery art in our culture, and 'live context' art in other cultures, will be looked at in more detail as we proceed.

We should find, as Christians, that an analysis of a culture and its sociology of knowledge in terms of power relations or governing myth is a valuable antidote to any sense of privilege or isolation the artist may unconsciously inherit from tradition. Learning how art is used to undergird and bolster a set of values, either in its conception and execution, or in its subsequent critical reception is a useful and necessary enterprise.

Placing art work, art talk, and art think back into the flow of society not only reminds artists of vulnerability, but also responsibility. Christians who want to address the vulnerabilities of official 'art history' through their work, or work in a more directly confrontational way will need to remain aware of the vulnerability of the artist in a society that has the capacity to absorb and recycle its most dissident elements. But we must also be aware of the problems of 'over contextualizing' our analysis of the artists and their work.

Problems can occur when some Christians, already in an uneasy relationship with the world and culture because of an inherited pietism, further simplify their world by over relying on large scale and sometimes simplified analysis of socio-cultural trends. The closest they come to directly engaging with the complexity of the art world and its history is to look at time lines, historical flowcharts and half page monochrome reproductions in some one else's book.

Because of this tendency among some of us to reductively analyze, or to avoid analysis altogether, then 'playing' and delighting in art 'for its own sake' may be an appropriate gesture for some of us moving into the arts. It could even be perceived as prophetic in its address to sterility and conformity of vision.

Playing and experimenting with media and its specific properties may be aspects of discipleship for someone whose vocation is in the arts, and perhaps it will work in opening the eyes of the church to what is possible when combinations of line, color, balance and density are appropriately judged, redeemed and transformed.

Work like this is not only worthy 'for its own sake' but also implicitly confronts those attitudes ingrained among some Christians that masquerade as piety but on closer examination mask a distrust of the world and a fear of the body and senses that is, as I have already suggested, completely alien to biblical Christianity. It is these issues, touched on in this initial overview that I want to explore more deeply in the remainder of this book.

3. How Can You Use Something That Leaks?

We have done a little bit of preliminary ground clearing in terms of looking at and thinking about art and art making from a Christian perspective. What I want to do now is suggest the basis for an underlying theology of creativity. In order to do so, I am going to 'frame' my arguments by sketching out some of the tensions that exist between cultures, within a culture, and within the church.

> *"I was favored with a rare chance of visiting a Korean village where beautiful lathed wood objects are made. When I got there after a long hard trip, I noticed at once by their workshop many big blocks of pine wood ready for the hand lathe. But to my great astonishment, all of them were still sap green and were by no means ready for immediate use. To my surprise a Korean craftsman took one of them, set it in a lathe and began forthwith to turn it. The pine block was so fresh that turning made a wet spray, which gave off a scent of resin. This perplexed me very much because it goes against common sense in lathe work. So! Asked the artisan, "Why do you use such green material? Cracks will come out pretty soon!" "What does it matter?" was the calm answer. I was amazed by this Zen monk like response. I felt sweat on my forehead. Yet l dared ask him, "How can you use something that leaks?"*
>
> *"Just mend it," was his simple answer.*
>
> *With amazement I discovered that they mend them so artistically and beautifully that the cracked piece seems better than the perfect one. So they do not mind whether it cracks or*

> *not. Our common sense is of no use for Koreans at all. Their*
> *way of making things is so natural that any man made rule*
> *becomes meaningless. They have neither attachment to the*
> *perfect piece nor to the imperfect.*"[16]

In this story is a picture of how the creativity of the craftsman is revealed in both making and repairing a piece of wooden folk art. If you like, this story portrays a marriage between the creative and the redemptive activities of the craftsman in the completion of a finished work. It could be said that the piece of work, and the craftsman's remarks about it reveal an overall philosophy of the artistic, and the beautiful.

In John 5, Jesus is challenged concerning a healing on the Sabbath. He points out (5:19-20) that He is simply following His Father's example. He uses the analogy of a child who observes a parent at work in a workshop and plays alongside, imitating the actions.

In Paul's letter to the Colossian church he identifies Christ as a primary agent in both creation and redemption (Colossians 1:15-22). Paul is writing to an infant church about the dangers of some heretical thinkers that tried to poison the purity and simplicity of the gospel of grace, and also compromise the doctrine of the Incarnation.

These thinkers were trying to enslave these new believers under a system of rules and regulations that appealed to 'the elemental principles' of ceremonial law and a philosophy founded on human tradition. Paul had to confront various false systems of belief that were offered to the infant churches as superior models of 'true Christianity.' Invariably, adherence to the Mosaic Law was being offered as either the only true way of appeasing God, or as part of an overall technology of initiation into the mysteries of 'true spirituality.'

Paul tries to remedy this by describing the exalted status of Christ, and His role in both creation and redemption. Both works are given equal weight, and have an equal degree of fittingness and perfection conferred upon them. They are seen as two facets of the ongoing dynamic of God's creativity. God creatively redeems.

The failure to grasp this relationship and continuity was a problem in the mind of the observer. We can see how the first author we quoted learned this in dialogue with a simple Korean craftsman. We have also seen how the religious authorities failed to grasp this as they argued with Jesus over a healing. As we move on in our consideration of tension and conflict between worldviews and cultures, I want us to do so with that dynamic curve between creation and redemption at the back of our minds.

Our first author refers to Zen Buddhism, which for us is a handy way of moving beyond the introductory material into the first 'layer' or 'dimension' of cosmic conflict, the war between cultures.

We are accustomed to thinking in stereotypes such as 'the mystic East' which posit a mystical, alien and largely impenetrable world view in stark contrast to the hard headed pragmatic West. I want to suggest two things.

Firstly, the two systems have some things in common. They both posit a superior 'self', somehow contemplatively or analytically disengaged from the world of appearances and contingent reality. I also want to suggest that the hard, pragmatic, technological, secular worldview traditionally associated with the West is grounded by faith in premises as relative in terms of ultimate truth, as those of a culture still saturated in nature mysticism.

If I understand correctly, the meditative traditions that are developing within the nature-based religions are looking to find or achieve 'ultimate reality' through contemplative absorption into whatever lies behind the world of appearances, concepts and observable phenomena. And yet it is impossible. To be human is to be engaged in that very realm. As Arthur Koestler points out in his book on creativity:

> Man is a symbol making animal. He constructs a symbolic model of outer reality in his brain, and expresses it by a second set of symbols in terms of words, equations, pigment or stone. All he knows directly and all he can directly do is perform bodily motions; the rest of his knowledge and means of expression is symbolical. To use a phrase coined by J. Cohen man has a metaphorical consciousness. Any attempt to get a direct grasp on naked reality is self defeating.[17]

It is the symbolic that links us to the sensed and experienced world. And it is the capacity to make and respond to symbols that makes us human. Whatever is conceived, enters our 'universe of discourse,' and becomes symbolically expressed. Even the Buddhist void becomes an image of the void.

That notwithstanding, I think it's worth observing that this disentangled self of detached meditation surfaced in the West as a self of detached observation. If in the East the suspicion over the interacting, suffering, thought- and image- making self, sent thinkers in pursuit of absorption into the world soul (from Jivatman to Atman), or total extinction in the clear light of Nirvana, then in the West, some thinkers tended to posit a superior thinking self that could neutrally handle the realm of facts.

We traditionally talk about the process of 'secularization' when thinking of this second cultural model of the self. This 'secular' mode of thinking abandons the transcendent, looks to science for ultimate explanations, and appeals to technology to enable man to progress towards a realization of all potentialities again.

Two quotes from Koestler explore the boundaries and expose the frailties of those assumptions. Koestler quotes Popper:

> *The old scientific ideal of epistime – of absolutely certain, demonstrable knowledge – has proved to be an idol. The demand for scientific objectivity makes it inevitable that every scientific statement must remain tentative forever. It may indeed be corroborated but every corroboration is relative to other statements, which again, are tentative. Only in our subjective experiences of conviction, in our subjective faith can we be 'absolutely certain'.* [18]

In so far as these subjective certainties find any expression at all in human hands, it will be a symbolic, creative expression:

> *The idea of progress (in science and any other field) is only about three centuries old; and only since the collapse of mechanistic science since the turn of the last century to dawn on the more far sighted among scientists that the unfolding of the secrets of nature was accompanied by a parallel process of infolding—that we were learning more and more about less and less. The more precise knowledge the physicist acquired the more ambiguous and oblique symbols he had to use to express it; he could no longer make an intelligible model of sub atomic reality, he could only allude to it by formal equations that have as much resemblance to reality as a 'telephone number to a subscriber.'* [19]

'Worldview' problems have had their impact on other fields of human endeavor, but as I am about to suggest, the same kind of ideas about progress alluded to above, the same kinds of specialization, with the same attendant problems of reference and language, can be traced in areas of recent art history in our culture.

Christian artists coming from a culture saturated with a 'secularist' worldview and getting together with Christian artists who come from a mystically rooted culture have a lot of room for dialogue. There are some areas of common ground between them, but there are also some striking differences in cultural tradition and expression. I believe that the first and main level of 'cosmic conflict', then, occurs between two cultures, and in that light I want to briefly explore some of the 'striking differences' in cultural tradition and expression that potentially enriches such dialogue.

The arts have taken different directions in different cultures. We, in the West, have a gallery and museum tradition surrounding the fine arts whereas other cultures still have the arts 'in place', integral to the social and spiritual life of the community. Let me give a very simple overview.

In the West we can look back over a long line of development in the area of the arts, going back to artistic values rooted variously in 'classical' virtues, in which Greek ideas of beauty and truth were channeled through art. As the worldviews changed so did the role of the arts, and many artists began to use their skills more in accurate rendition of the observable world. This gave way to a quest for inner truth that found symbolic outer expression, ranging from dream imagery through to various degrees of abstraction.

This ended in some artists paying attention only to those qualities and properties peculiar to the chosen medium and exploiting them. People are still arguing over whether or not this constituted a quest for ultimate purity, or a crisis of confidence. However, no matter how radical some artists tried to be they still ended up being absorbed back into the gallery and museum system. They needed a place to show the work, and also there would arise a body of attendant critical theory that helped 'accommodate' the artwork in and through the very act of interpretation.

Furthermore, the whole idea of a gallery, museum, and separate fine art, tradition, are fairly recent developments, developments that had an impact on how we in the West tend to look at cultural objects. If you like, these developments function as a conceptual 'framing' device, influencing the quantity and the quality of the attention we pay to those objects we call 'art.'

Art makers from other cultures on the other hand have a different history, and a different understanding of the role the arts play in their culture. For some the arts are still integrated into daily life, giving symbolic expression to the spiritual realities that the culture pays homage to. Those of us coming from cultures that have a separate 'fine art' tradition will be wrestling with the tension between our developing Christian world view and whatever underlying philosophy informs the current phase the arts are going through.

Christian artists coming from societies in which the arts are integral and functional, on the other hand, have a different set of problems. How have the art forms been 'traditionally' used? Are there direct spiritual and cultural implications for the form itself? How closely related are the artform and the worldview in a culture where the arts enhance everyday life rather than being shut away in a gallery somewhere? In what way does the integrated, functional esthetic support or prop up the traditional worldview? Is there a way of appropriating the form while subverting the meaning? So, two cultures clash, not only philosophically, but also in terms of the different roles that art plays in each culture.

A second layer of conflict occurs within a culture. In a culture like my own, we have to deal with the ongoing erosion between the 'fine art tradition' and popular culture, and the role signs, symbols and the mass media play in portraying a particular model of reality.

If the realm of the sciences and philosophy have undergone specialization, resulting in diminishing returns and arcane language, then, as I pointed out, in some ways so have the arts. Our separate high art tradition has filled the gallery with art that speaks a language that only a few people – other artists, and those educated in the arts – fully understand. The move beyond 'official' modern art into a 'Postmodern' gathering up of a variety of different styles, postures and critical theories merely heightens the sense of disorientation. Cultures like ours have moved on from the time when the arts were a source of social and spiritual nourishment for the people, as were the medieval mystery plays for example.

If the separate high art tradition represents an increasing abandonment of a sign-hungry public, in quest of some 'metaphysical' or 'purely material' absolute, then there are plenty of other forces happy to move in to address that deep felt social need for symbols and meaningful images, while pushing an agenda of their own.

It has been said that nature abhors a vacuum. Perhaps something similar can be said of the forces of the marketplace. Because we are metaphoric creatures, and symbol-hungry animals, some forces in our culture tend to wage war on us through what they feed us in terms of symbols and images.

Advertising, popular arts, even the seemingly dispassionate news media, all project a model of desire, or 'rightness' that we unconsciously gravitate towards. 'If you want to be considered OK, this is what you should want to be like.' The power of images is very evident. Turn on the TV set and watch the impact of US TV shows, *Miami Vice* or *Dallas.*

Visit the tourist section of a developing world country and see how the 'image' has been set up to attract people and their money. Remember the way Adolf Hitler used speeches, film, uniforms, and mass rallies to provide a symbolic vocabulary that would move the German people to action. Here we have examples of media manipulation and symbolic gestures with real political and historical results.

What happens today? Think of the popular depiction of other races or of women. Does the manner of depiction in a given situation enhance and dignify their humanity? What is depicted as a desirable role model? The apostle Paul speaks in Romans 12 of renewing the mind and not being conformed to the passing age. The second level of conflict therefore, is when the arts are co-opted by forces of alienation and domination, in order to use and manipulate the God-given 'metaphoric/symbolic' consciousness of man, through powerful images and symbols that redefine for him what is real, what is normal and what is desirable.

In some cultures we might identify this at work in the worship of idols, the observation of ceremonies and rituals, trance events and other things. In other cultures we recognize this in what we believe, what we feel 'free' to purchase, or how we see ourselves in the light of a cultural norm.

So what we have here are two dimensions of cosmic conflict. There is a clash between cultures, and the different way the cultures view the arts, and then the war within a culture, and how images and symbols are used at a popular level to wage such a war. The final dimension of the conflict occurs in the church and the heart and the conscience of the individual Christian.

We have already touched on some of the questions about the arts and the worldview they operate in. I hope I have demonstrated that the problem is a serious one, not only in terms of folk arts and spirit events, but also in terms of fine art that lost its voice while crying in the wilderness of secularization.

I believe that the church should seek to nurture the artist, and honor the symbol-making and image-bearing capacity of everyone, on one hand seeking to avoid hostility and misunderstanding, and on the other hand not succumbing to the temptation to glibly exploit those capacities.

Finally, we must talk a little about the church and the arts. If our culture at large is struggling under the weight of secularization, specialization, and a closed fine art tradition, then sections of the church are still approaching the arts with a suspicion that has more to do with Plato and Aristotle than John or Paul.

For Plato the artist made an imperfect copy of a world that in turn was an imperfect copy of an ultimate reality. Aristotle tried to rehabilitate the dramatic arts by asserting that somehow to witness the dramatic spectacle had a purging effect on the soul.

While the church is very vocal in its protest against the forces of secularization, some of its arguments against art draw water from the same river. The arts become a beast of burden, valuable only in terms of how much of a message they can be made to carry. For many of us, we have to firstly come to terms with art as 'art' before we can really understand its potentialities in a larger cultural context.

Dorothy L. Sayers has written of a 'complete revolution of ideas' that should have occurred at Pentecost, calling into question the older philosophical models of reality, and the approaches to art that sprang from those models.

She goes on to point out that art rooted in a trinitarian and incarnational theology should also be free from any drab utilitarianism and stern moralism borrowed lock stock and barrel from non-biblical sources and married to world-denying 'know nothing' form of pietism.

There is nothing wrong with the idea of art having its place, and being useful. However, for art to be truly useful and socially relevant it may have to be weaned away from former slave owners, and allowed to stretch and play a little for its own sake, while we work out a dynamic theology that clears the way for, and then undergirds, a greater sense of freedom.

I believe that work like this in the church of our own culture will prepare the ground for achieving an understanding of the complex relationship between art and spiritual values we find in other cultures. There is much work to be done.

Some of us will feel called to challenge the church's limited vision. Others will feel the need to look for ways of protecting the tender conscience of the individual believer. These will be issues in every culture, from the secularized post-Christian west, to those cultures still governed by a completely different worldview and spiritual perspective.

In looking at these issues, we have traveled a long way from the story of the Korean craftsman. But I believe that our recognition that there is no conflict between God's creative activity and His redeeming activity sets the stage for our brief exploration of the conflict between cultures, the conflict within a culture, and the battle within the church and also within the individual believer's conscience.

Hopefully this exploration begins to clear the way for our understanding, appreciating and making of art to the glory of God, whatever our cultural background. Another step in clearing the way takes place as we look around for examples of the kind of creativity that could, or should be possible in the light of the ideas talked about above. A good place to start our search is the Bible.

4. Nothing More Than Dirt?

Again I will begin with a story. I read recently that many people were protesting about the cleaning and restoration of the Sistine chapel, because, it seems, that the colors in the original artwork were much more vibrant and lively than generations of viewers had been led to believe. The muted colors and the pale tones that many had drawn spiritual and emotional sustenance from turned out to be nothing more than dirt. The artist, apparently, had intended something quite different, and it was all there, if you took the trouble to clean the layers of accumulated grime away.

I sometimes wonder when we look at the Bible how many vibrant and lively colors are there waiting for us to discover them. And I wonder sometimes if we are approaching the material itself, or the layers of grime that have been built up over the years.

When we talk about art and creativity from a Christian perspective, I believe that there is much we can learn by simply going back to the Bible itself, not so much for 'proof texts' for or against art, but more for examples of the kinds of liberty and creativity the writers themselves explored. In an earlier chapter I suggested four ways of looking at developments in recent art. Now I want to take a similar approach to the Bible.

In Genesis, in the psalms, and elsewhere, there is inspired writing celebrating the goodness of the created order. There is also talk, in sometimes startling metaphor and imagery, about the responsiveness of the created order to God, and celebration of the mystery and wonder of man, and the senses. We notice three things.

First, there is a created order. In Genesis 2 we see a primary relationship between esthetic and moral values. The love of beauty, and love of truth are together. The true God declares the handiwork truly good.

Second, there is an equally complex 'appreciator' of this given order in 'man.' Not only are we equipped to explore and delight in what is all around us – we are also, according to the Psalmist, able to turn our focus inward upon the complexity and the mystery of the 'self.' We are placed here to appreciate the sensed environment (and our sense of 'being') in the context of a working relationship with God.

Psalmist and prophet also write of the created order in responsive relationship with God. The prophet Isaiah writes creatively about the response-relationship between created and Creator (Isaiah 55:10-13) using the startling metaphors of singing mountains and applauding trees.

Finally, it is worth observing that some authors have even pointed out that the early Old Testament materials, in talking about a personal God and an orderly creation, were written to distinctly challenge some of the mythologies of the nations that Israel moved among. Even the 'good work' can, at some levels, have an implicit apologetic.

A second characteristic of creativity in biblical thinking is evidenced in what some of the Old Testament prophets do. There is harsh sounding poetic denunciation, and bizarre dramatic performance aimed at an idolatrous or complacent Israel. Jeremiah wore and then buried a girdle, leaving it to rot underground to provide a graphic image of Israel's true state before God. He also went down to a potter's house and learned something from both the wheel and the sun hardened clay. He made his point by smashing a pot.

Ezekiel drew a scale model of the city on a tile and then surrounded it with models of destruction. Isaiah walked about naked, and Hosea married a prostitute. The prophets of the Old Testament used a variety of creative attention-grabbing means to challenge the nation God had made a covenant with. However, they did not restrict themselves to using radical theater to confront corporate sin. Nathan the prophet used a story to challenge an individual, David, concerning the misuse of his position of authority to license adultery and arrange a murder.

The prophets confronted Israel concerning its spiritual harlotry; a complete capitulation to the spirit of the age. They also addressed Israel's complacent over-reliance on the formality of its own spiritual traditions, and in David's case, Nathan used narrative to depict and implicitly condemn the misuse of power for gain at the expense of the powerless. These were the things the prophets graphically addressed, using performance, poetry and storytelling.[20]

The biblical writers not only celebrated God's order of creation, but they also wrote of the various orders of imagery at work in God's plan of redemption. The great themes of creation, recreation and restoration can be traced from Genesis through Revelation. They echo throughout God's mighty work with Israel, and then in Christ on behalf of the church.

Not only are these themes woven through the biblical narrative, there is also God's redemptive imagery at work in the natural created environment. According to the early chapters of Genesis one of the earliest covenants was established with Noah, through the sign of a rainbow. This covenant formed the background of Paul's argument with the natives of Lystra in the Book of Acts.

The biblical writers also began to prepare the ground for the coming Messiah. There were various kinds of symbolic indicators of the person and the work of Christ, 'seed metaphors' scattered throughout the Old Testament. Firstly, there were the characteristics, some of the attributes, and some of the 'callings of God' in the lives of Old Testament characters, such as Joseph, Moses, Joshua, David, Solomon and Melchizedek.

As they lived out their lives within a particular culture that was being impacted by the unfolding revelation of God's covenant love, the stories of those lives contributed to that unfolding revelation as they were recorded by the Old Testament writers.

There is imagery in some of the provision God made for Israel on its long march through the wilderness. The bread from heaven and the water from the stricken rock are two examples. Then there is the giving of the law, and the institution of various kinds of sacrifices, sin offerings and ceremonial purifications.

We can find evidences of the kinds of ceremonial cleansing that the death of Jesus would perfect in the dove offerings of the poor, the purification sacrifice of the red heifer, and the 'sending out' of the sin-laden scapegoat into the wilderness. We can also look at the crafted details of the tabernacle for more clues of the one to come, and pick up Jesus' own reference to the brazen serpent of Numbers 21 as a foreshadowing of His work. [21]

Then there are the forms, in the actual genres of literature. We can observe the 'redemption' theme at the heart of Old Testament stories like the book of Ruth. Startling drama co-exists with concrete realism at the heart of Jesus' parable.[22] Then there are the literary and dramatic shapes of the Gospel accounts themselves.[23]

Paul also employed allegory and narrative to undergird his arguments to the Galatians and the Corinthians. Old Testament writers borrowed from the poetic forms of their neighbors for their psalms and songs in praise of the true God. They also told stories that centered on the themes of retrieval and redemption.

Paul and others drew upon rabbinic methods and traditions of interpretation to open up the doors between the Old Testament and the revelation of Christ,[24] and gospels and epistles were set out in literary forms congenial to the potential Greek and Roman reading audience.[25]

Jesus Himself drew upon the 'old and the new' combining narrative, sign, and prophetic performance, in creatively demonstrating the meaning of God's love to an individual, a nation, and a world.

The fourth strain of creativity is found in those sections of biblical material dubbed 'apocalyptic.'[26] These writers symbolically described the end of history and the coming of the true God to establish a totally new order.

Whether the writers are describing a vast international or cosmic conflict, or talking about all the nations flocking to worship the true God in His holy mountain, or setting out to depict a totally new order in which lambs and wolves play together, they are working in that context that stretches inspired creativity in new ways, in its depictions of the collapse of history, the birth pangs of a new phase of God's purposes. And next to the apocalyptic we have Paul's hints to the Corinthians that we see through a glass darkly, but a time is coming of total communion and utter transparency.

In earlier chapters we looked at Christian responses to some of the major trends in recent modern art, and tried to consider the ways in which Christians could make art in the light of these trends, and also in the light of the various traditions of creativity within the church. We also went on to explore some of these issues in a 'cross-cultural' setting. I want to take the discussion further by seeing what we can learn from the precedents established by the Biblical writers, as briefly outlined above.

1). Artists can engage in skillful depiction of the seen and heard world. They can also organize seen and heard materials, colors, sounds, into an artistic totality, even using some measure of abstraction rooted in the perceptual and sensual order. Whether in painting or sculpture or even environmental installation, artists can bring idea and creativity to bear upon work that celebrates. And, of course, like the celebratory materials of the Bible, it will assert a different range of values in its depiction, and even its abstraction. It will posit a different order against those artworks that seek to abstract themselves from all reference and history.

It will also challenge those approaches to art that make the human form divine, and root all their subsequent standards of beauty and perfection from this initial idolatry. So there is a Christian work to be done, in the depiction and celebration of the natural world, the human form, and even in abstract use of form, material, color and weight.

2). We need artwork that condenses into artistic form an address to a prevailing human problem (i.e. a failure to live up to our own values) or a particular cultural one (our version of idolatry, or religious complacency). What are our idols, and what would be a contemporary way of confronting them? How can an artist effectively challenge our insularity and complacency? What is there to be challenged?

I believe that Christian artists can take on the prophetic mandate in their work, and confront more deeply than others who try. As I suggested earlier, other prophets, be they anti artists calling for the end of the corrupt gallery system, or punk rockers declaring pop music dead, end up getting absorbed back into the very system they try and criticize. Still others prophesy against the entrenchments of capitalism, the Enlightenment, western civilization or whatever, but they prophesy from a false basis, the wrong god, or their own rage.

3). How do we 'redemptively' handle 'redemptive' materials as they come to us in the form of signs, symbols and narrative? What works for us as a redemption story, or a Christ figure? What images can be brought in from outside our frame of immediate reference and turned into effective symbols? (Many of Jesus's signs dealt with individuals who for one reason or another were placed 'outside' …the Samaritan woman, the woman with the issue of blood…Matthew a tax collector…a 'good' Samaritan.

What would be appropriate as a contemporary equivalent, sufficiently 'outside,' and sufficiently a sign? How do we charge what we import with new meaning? What is our 'brazen serpent?' And what about the overall shape of our chosen artistic form? Are the structures themselves essential to the message they 'contain?'

Do we rob a story of its redemptive potential if we explain its 'spiritual' meaning? Remember, we are talking about human beings placed in a relational responsive network. Jesus, quoting Isaiah, talked about not explaining his parables in case the Pharisees worked them out too easily. Is there something about the 'whole person' response to art that sets up the ground for God to move?

If figuring it out is part of the process (as it was for Nicodemus, in John 3:1 –2 with Jesus' talk of 'born again' and the 'serpent lifted up') what is available to the Christian to work with? How does a Christian behave truly redemptively within the context and the medium? Which questions are to be left unanswered? Which symbols and parables are to remain unexplained? How do we establish the boundaries?

Other Christ figures are out there, too. Phantoms who have no history, who were never human. They offer to lead you to a promised land of racial purity, or a cosmic new age of good vibrations. And these other gospels have their artists, too.

4). What, for today's artist, is an appropriate way of depicting the frailty and contingency of human history? Is it in the self-taught visionary paintings of people like Howard Finster? Is it in the 'Peaceable Kingdom' sequence of the Quaker painter Edward Hicks, who depicted lions, lambs, fields, and trees in harmonious bliss? Or the playful, colorful work of Marc Chagall?

What we all fear, I suppose, is the possibility of a 'Christian' Star Wars movie, or a theme park based on the book of Revelation. What we actually need are those artists who can stare into, and unflinchingly depict, the breakdown of human history. We need artists who can develop a symbolic vocabulary for their work that awakens intuitions in the eye, ear, and heart, of another totally different order, an order that is not only possible, but because of the kindness and power of God, inevitable.

We also need artists who like Paul have looked into the smoked glass of this present reality, and can somehow, through the manipulation of color, line and space, awaken in us that heaven-seeded hunger for purity and transparency and knowing as we are known. Some modern, non-Christian artists have glimpsed that, and tried to register that sense of yearning and loss in the abstraction of their work. Others, as I pointed out in chapter one, have insisted that the work of the artist is to so purify the perceptions of the hearer and viewer, that everything from that point on can be appreciated as art. Art, life, chaos and order simply become arbitrary labels.

In order to further our exploration of a Christian perspective on creativity and the arts, we are going to take some time to focus on a particular gospel story and see what it has to tell us.

5. Freedom, Power and Creativity

Everything we have looked at so far has challenged us, I hope, to re-think our basic concepts about the arts. We have looked at the arts and the Bible, the freedom of Christians, what art is 'good for', and the value and necessity of creativity in thinking and discipleship. I want now to examine one well-known biblical story to see what it can tell us about freedom, power and creativity.

The Bible talks about the idea of a supremely creative God, and I think when we think in terms of supreme creativity we think in terms of creativity without limitation—a being who is creatively free to do anything. This is why the question about God creating a rock that He cannot lift is so absurd: because we cannot conceive of a supremely creative being having the power to voluntarily impose a limitation on the exercise of that power. One of the reasons we find that hard to fathom is because in our culture we treat creativity and infinite freedom as self-contained abstract categories rather than as characteristics of a personal God. And these categories are disengaged in our thinking from the world of experience and reference.

We can go back to the roots of Western philosophy with Plato's realm of eternal truths above and beyond the world of appearances, or we can come into today's perplexing 'postmodern' era in which the revolution in communication and information transmission has opened windows onto a variety of landscapes. Different cultures, and completely different pictures of reality are just an electronic signal away.

Whether we are chained in the darkness of Plato's cave, or lost in the global village there is an uncritical assumption that absolute truth and absolute freedom, if they exist at all, lie outside the realm of appearances, and the culturally and linguistically specific 'prison house' of description. And so for God who personifies ultimate truth and freedom to choose to demonstrate truth and freedom by voluntarily entering the realm of appearance and description is a challenge to our entire worldview.

When we explore the Gospel story of the three temptations of Christ in the wilderness we find a discussion about the medium God has chosen for the recreation of the World. It of necessity involves two kinds of limitations that God the artist has chosen to work with.

Firstly it involves entering this particular creation, and then it involves taking on a particular cultural context. If you like, not just taking on the medium itself, but also the history of work and response to that work within a particular genre. If I announced I was going to take up landscape painting, not only would I need to familiarize myself with the canvas and the properties of a chosen medium, oils, acrylics etc, but also with the laws of observation and perspective, and the different effects of light.

I would also want to gain some acquaintance with the genre. I might want to familiarize myself with the work of Constable, Turner, and so on. In order to work effectively as an artist within a given range of subject matter, I would choose not only a medium, but also the historical cultural context.

Now for God the chosen medium was not only a man (as opposed to the universal 'Man') but also the history and culture of Israel. The letter to the Hebrews talks about the different modes of revelation used prior to the coming of the Son. God's sovereignty is not compromised by expressive diversity. As Paul pointed out to the church at Rome, the whole created order bears witness to the power of God.

Then, as we discussed earlier, there are the Old Testament prophets and the symbolism in the sacrifices and the tabernacle. All these things found their fulfillment and resolution in the chosen medium of the Son who takes on the limitations of material and culture to express God's love.

These temptations, therefore, are an attempt to compromise God's choice of medium, and also to get him to step outside of His chosen cultural frame of reference. The adversary firstly tempts Christ to turn stone into bread. Jesus' refusal had nothing to do with inability, and everything to do with remaining 'in context' so that bread, rather than being mere substance in His hands, could remain free to be a symbol.

As Jesus endures forty days in the wilderness He symbolically echoes the experience of Israel and its forty years of wandering. To 'break character' and create bread for Himself, would have rendered His identification less than total.

He would have been fully human, except for that one weak moment when He used His divine power to step out of character and eat. To create bread for others would have only addressed one level of their need. And God was working on a total recreation.

Reread the story of the feeding of the five thousand. In John's account He reminded the crowd that was asking Him to repeat the performance that what he had done with the bread was intended to point beyond material need ('Why do you work for the bread that perishes?') and even beyond cultural and historical symbol ('Your Fathers ate bread in the wilderness and died.') back to Himself as the 'true bread that had come down from heaven.' (See John Chapter 6.)

Jesus was pointing out that He was the source of created reality, and also the meaning of the entire symbol system of their culture, and, furthermore, if they wanted to experience true life, they should go to Him and drink His blood and eat His flesh. He would have lost the right to say that if he had deconstructed a stone and turned it into bread in the wilderness.

In Luke 24 Jesus walks alongside two disciples on the Emmaus road. In doing so, He is able to discuss the Old Testament with them. When they stop for a meal, Jesus breaks the bread and this opens their eyes. Their hearts burned within them on the road as he walked and explained. How could the bread breaking have been so revealing of Jesus if 'bread' had not retained its integrity as a sign? How could their hearts have burned within them if He had not walked? And how could he say that He truly walked if he had not gone hungry, in solidarity with Israel, in the wilderness?

The second temptation, to throw himself from the roof of the temple, was not only to test the providence of God, but also to garner the popular allegiance of the people through a powerful display of the spectacular. We can refer to it as spectacle without substance, a display that, as fantastic as it appears, virtually has no relevance to the real issues of the context.

When the art world becomes fascinated with the new for the sake of newness, and caught up with novelty and 'flash' it signals two things. Firstly there is a failure of a cultural or a historical tradition to provide a basis for contemporary meaning. Secondly we as people prefer the glib, the instant, and the vacuous, because it makes no emotional, moral or intellectual demands upon us. We remain 'uncontaminated' by thought and deep feeling. We 'keep' our freedom.

Now for Jesus to jump from the temple roof and survive would have gotten him some popular support, no doubt. Everyone loves a hero. And even that kind of heroism in the name of Israel would have found its followers. They might have crowned him king on the spot, and held their breath waiting for the Roman government to collapse. But it is one thing to create a spectacle by jumping off the roof of the temple, it is quite another to go into the temple, drive out all the animals, turn over the money tables and call the temple authorities a bunch of common criminals who have defiled the intents and purposes of God.

Jesus brings some substance to his statements by dismantling the whole sacrificial and 'temple tax' paying machinery from within, and when asked for His credentials, talks about tearing down the temple and rebuilding it in about half a week.

Again, Jesus is offering himself as the true sacrifice, and the true currency for paying God, and in this action and subsequent statement Jesus (according to John's sequencing of events) sets in motion the chain of action and reaction that would result in Him being tried and executed for political sedition (He challenged the authority of Caesar), blasphemy (He called himself equal with God), and desecration of the temple (He was heard publicly encouraging his followers to profane and tear down the temple). Then, to cap it all, He rises from the dead.

The misunderstandings and misinterpretations that the religious authorities of the time read into Jesus' words and actions contributed to their resolve to stop Him at any cost. It was in the act of stopping Him that they set in motion the very things that made His words and actions ultimately true and ultimately effective.

The foolishness of God, according to the apostle Paul, is wiser than the wisdom of men. Jesus remained 'in control' of His medium by cleansing the temple rather than leaping from its roof. Again, none of this would have been possible if Jesus had succumbed to the second temptation and compromised His use of the chosen medium of created reality, a particular cultural history, and the real need of His audience.

Finally, in the temptation to bow to the Devil and be given access to the kingdoms of the world, Jesus is offered all that He came for, but on someone else's terms. Salvation becomes a commodity, an option within a pantheon of options. It all becomes one. The choices become illusory because, beneath the surface appearance of diversity, there is the hard reality of total uniformity.

There is no real choice left. It is like a phony 'price war' between two supermarkets owned by the same parent company. It is like four breakfast cereal companies arguing about who has the most nutritional value in a series of television commercials, and then it being revealed that the four companies are subdivisions of a parent company that has also diversified its holdings by buying the TV station the commercials appear on.

As we have suggested in previous chapters some artists have tried to resist this 'commodification' by extracting themselves from the world of reference and appearance, and focussing in on a marriage of pure material arrangements and pure ideas. If something in their work was recognizable, it was a joke, or intended to be an ironic statement about popular culture or the 'official' history of art.

Jesus on the other hand, the supreme artist, risked precisely the things many of today's artists shy away from. He engaged with us both in terms of material and a particular cultural and historical reality.

The temptations that Jesus faced in the wilderness centered on compromising His involvement with his chosen medium by reminding Him what he was purely and sovereignly free to do with stones, jumping from roofs, and entering a gentleman's agreement. The Temptation story, seen in this light, also serves to remind us about some of the misconceptions about creativity and freedom that lie deep within our particular worldview.

In order to go further in our exploration of a Christian perspective on creativity and the arts, we need to look at our relationship to our physical 'selves' and our relationship to our cultural environment and its worldview in the light of Paul's remarks to the church in Rome about the necessity of a 'living sacrifice.'

6. Living Sacrifice/ Transformed Mind

When I shared the Picasso 'Guernica' story with some students at Biola University one autumn, we came up with the concept of 'disembodied thinking' as a metaphor for one of the problems at the root of how many of us think about and go about making art. I hope what is being discussed here starts to clear the way past the obstacle of 'disembodied thinking' and opens up fruitful lines of dialogue, inquiry, and also goads more of us into informed action.

Truly 'embodied' thinking will locate itself in our other earlier metaphor of gift exchange, not so much (initially) in terms of the arts in society, but more in terms of the gift of God's only son, and our response to that gift. Paul neatly sums up the relationship between God's gift and our response in Ephesians 2: 6-10. On the basis of God's wonderful gift of His son to us, we are set free, not merely to spin in anarchic self-defeating circles, but free to creatively fulfill the purposes God equipped and designed us for before time. Our fulfillment of those purposes is what we 'offer back' to God.

It is this 'exchange' that enriches and deepens our experience of fellowship with God. We begin to experience something of the 'network' or 'community' that Jesus talks about and prays for (according to the Gospel of John) during the 'Upper Room' sequence (John 13 – 17).

Paul also talks about our response to God's wonderful gift in Romans 12:1 – 3. Firstly he appeals to his listeners 'by the mercies of God'. He has spent eleven chapters of this epistle systematically rehearsing these mercies as they are evidenced in God's maintenance of the created order, and God's dealings with the nations. Having argued for the centrality and supreme relevance of the work of Christ, Paul then talks about 'presenting our bodies' as a 'living sacrifice.' He talks about this step as a necessary guard against being unduly 'conformed to the world' and also as preparation for 'transformation through the renewing of the mind'.

I now want to briefly look at this sequence of images in order to see what we can learn about our place as Christians in thinking about and making art in our present culture.

'Present your bodies.' Paul is arguing against two stumbling blocks in the culture of the time, that, incidentally are still with us. Firstly, he is arguing against the undue intellectualism and philosophical mysticism of the time that would divorce spiritual concerns from the 'lower level' of physical reality. Spiritual truth involves the whole self, including the physical body.

Secondly, he is challenging the orgiastic indulgences of physical appetites practiced by some, either for hedonistic pleasure, or as a quest for 'spiritual truth' via the road of excess. Unfortunately some of us spend so much time agreeing with Paul on the things we should avoid (an undue distrust of the body still leaks into some areas of 'Christian' thought) that we fail to grasp the positive implications of what Paul is asking.

This 'body' we give back to God, is the primary ground of our observed and experienced relationship with the rest of creation. On the basis of our observation and experience, we come to understand movement.

Think of the infant. How we see the world change as we move away into an emerging separate identity. Think of the exploration of the emerging self that goes on in the creative play that takes place in that newly realized space. Think of the physical and social identity that forms as we scribble, as we experience the act of drawing.

Our relationship with the world changes as we learn to balance, and walk. We internalize rhythms. Whether it be a buried memory of the heartbeat, or the daily cycles of sleeping and waking, we start to perceive an organization of time, and from there we abstract rhythms that feed into our response to the world, in singing and dancing.

We see things. Images at first, but then we learn, through comparison to let things stand for other things. Symbols and imagery. We begin to understand by comparing our observations, the larger patterns of rhythm and symbols. We build ourselves up to an understanding of analogy, symbolism and metaphor.

Now, in reference to Paul's words, the way some of us go about 'sacrificing the body' with no regard for the rich network of relationships the body places us in has more in common with Jesus's parable of the wicked servant who buried his talent!

Paul asks for a living 'whole person' sacrifice, that would necessarily involve placing that rich network of potential play and affective imaginings rooted in physical experience back into the hands of a creative, redeeming God. Also, this sacrifice, being 'our reasonable service' has to be a considered, thought-out one. It is not something we go about mechanically. Neither sterile ceremonialism nor undue sentimentality will suffice.

Unless there is a complete giving back to God of our whole person, including the body through which we experience, and creatively organize that experience into something 'new', then we will not have a sufficient basis for avoiding being unduly shaped by the pressures of our social environment.

Paul addresses this next when he challenges his hearers to be 'no longer conformed to the world, but transformed through the renewing of your mind.'

It's beyond the scope of this book to explore in any detail the way in which Rome maintained its status as the absolute central site of imperial power through the mass media of the time. I feel that such an exploration is going to be crucial to any larger expansion on this lecture, but for the time being I simply want to focus in on our contemporary equivalent.

This 'world' (especially in this twentieth century electronic global village) tries to build and communicate a 'total world picture' that is a (largely unacknowledged or recognized) attempt to replicate the benefits of a relationship with God without the acknowledgement of God. (Romans 1:16). It is an attempt to heal the split between ourselves and God, between our 'self' and the 'world' and between 'mind' and 'body.' It is these fault lines that run through our thinking and doing, and the world tries to use its technology to heal the wound.

It looks for explanations in psychology, in materialist and economic analyses of history, or it points back to the collapse of classical values and a Golden Age, no longer with us. So the world attempts to use technology and media both in diagnosis and healing of the sick situation.

It tries to construct this image in three ways:

In our context it first offers a false model of 'individuality', one that is 'free' from the context of accountability to God and neighbor. This 'freedom' consists of being held captive by powerful delusions of 'authenticity' or even potential 'divinity' (everything from 'you are the captain of your fate, 'to 'we're all one') symbolically expressed by our surrounding culture.

Everything from literature and art that celebrates the 'cult of the individual' and the meaninglessness of the Universe, through to what flashes across our screens in soap operas, game shows and MTV is part of this model. So also are the cosmic rainbows and the tinkling chimes of the so-called 'New Age Movement'.

Hand in hand with this false model of individuality is secondly a false model of 'community'. The necessary and powerful ideals that configure this 'community' and keep it 'in shape' are also filtered through the media and the arts. We are all deeply hungry for images and symbols. Somebody once said that Man is a symbol-making animal. It is part of what makes us identifiably human.

We have seen that our capacity for making and thinking symbolically is grounded in the body. Now we can see that as individuals and a community, fallen and in flight from God, we are in many ways controlled by the power we attribute to the symbols we create. As we allow this 'world' or 'passing age' to assume the status of 'ultimate reality,' it looks for effective means of reinforcing its central status in our lives.

It does this through the arts and the media. Everything from the dominant power structures that control the political realities, the depiction and designation of stereotypical roles, ethnic, sexual, through to 'idealized pictures of romantic love' finds expression within this model.[27]

As well as a powerful but false environment of 'freedom' through the media that is believed to be 'ultimately real' there is, thirdly, a 'false history' that is a selective reading of the 'story so far' which points its constituents back to 'progress' or necessary 'balances of power' as keys to understanding and maintaining the freedoms outlined above. It paints a picture of the way things were, and why things are the way they are, and how they ought to be. It is of course, a selective, biased reading.

I am suggesting that the manipulation of the media plays a large part in keeping the illusion going. It does this by appealing to the imaginative and symbolic dimensions of our lives, dimensions rooted largely in the body. I have already pointed out that to merely ignore, or dismiss the realm of the body was one of the very things that Paul argued against. It would follow, therefore, that a mere distrust of the arts or media is also implicitly addressed by Paul's argument. Jesus himself warned of the dangers of merely leaving a house 'swept clean' and left empty.

In Romans 12:1-2 Paul also yokes together the idea of a 'sacrificed body' with a 'transformed, renewed mind.' While all the implications of this transformation and renewal are open to discussion, I believe we can initially say three things.

This renewal necessarily involves taking on the 'servant/crucified mind' that Paul points the church at Philippi to when holding up the example of Christ's Incarnation and sacrifice in Philippians. It also opens up for us new dimensions of perception and imagination.

First, our eyes will gradually open to the mechanisms of persuasion and reinforcement filtered through the arts and media in our own culture. We will start to pay attention to what is being advertised and how it is being advertised. We will look beyond the supposed neutrality of the photographic image to what it was the photographer chose to focus on, and also to the context in which the photograph is being used. We will pay closer attention to the news, in an age when news readers are selected on the basis of camera presence, and news is managed for us in information bites.

Even in the fine arts, we can look at the way modern art is absorbed back into the ebb and flow of the status quo. Art that is about nothing else but material processes might be 'pure' but it is also non-threatening. Art that attempts to criticize the debased culture of the mass media remains reliant upon that culture for its exposure, and sometimes gets assimilated by the very thing it set out to challenge. Art that celebrates the absolute freedom of the artist sometimes ends up as a shop window for the political system that allows certain closely controlled harmless forms of 'absolute freedom.'

Second, we will 'die to' the inherited notions of cultural superiority that impact our understanding of the diversity of artistic expression in other cultures.

We unconsciously inherit a certain way of looking at things to do with the arts and culture.

We inherit and internalize standards of grace and beauty that are not absolute and universally valid, but have specific historical, cultural and in some cases political origins. These standards and inherited attitudes are maintained in some ways by the way the gallery and museum system arranges and exhibits artifacts from our own cultural history. It guides us in a selective reading of that history.

Our attitude to the arts of other cultures can also in some way be influenced by how a museum chooses to mount such an exhibition, and what it chooses to release as information, via catalog notes etc. It is possible to mount a show of art from other cultures in such a way so as to reinforce our own sense of cultural superiority.

Having a 'crucified mind' is going to involve stepping back from those inherited notions and learning to appreciate human creativity as it finds expression in a diversity of cultures. We will also come to grips with the diverse roles art plays in these cultures. Not all art forms in other cultures end up being separated out into galleries and museums for detached aesthetic contemplation.

In some cultures, like Bali, there is not even a word for art. The people there live in an ongoing 'gesture of balance' between spiritual and material reality. All that is done 'artistically' is to help maintain that balance. This includes everything from simple roadside rice and flower offerings to elaborate ceremonial dances, and the mysterious *wayang kulit* shadowplay.

Third, as we read through the startling parables and symbolic actions of Jesus with new eyes, then new images, imagery, ways of thinking and handling symbols will begin to take shape within us.

Jesus told parables and stories not as the rabbis did, to uphold the centrality and validity of the Law and the oral tradition, but in order to point back to Himself, and to the burning love of God, and to the coming Kingdom.

When Jesus cleansed the temple, he not only dismantled the sacrificial system from inside out, but he offered Himself as the reality that the system symbolically pointed to. When Nicodemus asked Jesus to explain the meaning of being 'born from above' Jesus reminded him of the story in Numbers 21, of the backslidden Children of Israel in the wilderness receiving healing for their snakebites by looking upon an uplifted serpent of brass.

At a party celebrating the return of Lazarus from the dead, Jesus commended Mary for her symbolic gesture of anointing his feet with perfumed oil. When Judas criticized the cost effectiveness of such a gesture in the face of so much pressing social need, Jesus replied in such a way as to point to His impending departure, using a brief quotation from Deuteronomy 15 ('the poor are always with you') to hint at a relationship between the central purpose of His departure and the special year of release from all debts in Israel.

We have seen three examples of crucified mind thinking. *1: Waking up* to the mechanisms of control and reinforcement through art and media in our own culture. *2: Dying* to notions of cultural superiority, and learning to appreciate diversity of cultural forms and expression. *3:Coming alive* to the imaginative, symbolic, narrative and artistic patterns available in the life of Jesus. They are simply the first step we must take after we have heeded Paul's injunction to no longer be conformed to the world.

I believe this exploration of what Paul had to say to the Romans helps us clear away some of the stumbling blocks and enables us to move deeper into a truly Christian understanding of the role artists can potentially play in the community.

Now we need to consider some other things. We might learn new ways of thinking about art and culture(s) by reflecting on the dynamic relationship between creation and redemption in the overall purposes of God. Art grounded in the overall examples we find among the Biblical writers might be liberated.

Our artwork might be further liberated as we grasp the relationship between a 'living sacrifice' and a 'transformed mind.' Is it possible that art making and art theory might have a contribution to make in other areas of Christian thinking, for example in helping us wrestle with some of the central issues of our faith?

7. Where Language Ends?

Up until now, we have tried to clear a way through the wilderness of modern art and cultural attitudes, using the Bible, and then more specifically the apostle Paul's words to the church at Rome as our guiding light. I want to press on from there, and look inward.

If in our last chapter, we laid the groundwork to begin moving out into culture, then in this chapter I want to focus on what the arts have to say to the church about some of its central beliefs.

While I think we can agree that there are some tremendous potentials for Christian working and thinking in the arts, I also want to ask if there are ways in which a renewed and applied understanding of the arts can help us not only communicate elements of the Christian message but also get a grasp on some of the foundation stones upon which that message is built.

I believe that one of the primary values the gift of art has for us today is helping us in our understanding of the gift of God's love. In fact, I believe that the arts are able in some ways to serve us better in this area than some other forms of language. It has been observed by more than one writer that our methods of explanation often end up impacting at some level the very reality we are trying to explain. Arthur Koestler explains:

> *"Words are essential tools for formulating and communicating thoughts, and putting them into the storage of memory; but words can also become snares, decoys or straight jackets. A great number of basic verbal concepts in science have turned out to be at various times both tools and traps: for instance 'time'. 'space'. 'mass', 'force', 'weight', 'ether', 'corpuscle', 'waves in the physical sciences; 'purpose', 'will', 'sen-*

sation', 'consciousness', 'conditioning'- in psychology; 'limits
'continuity', 'countability', 'divisibility' in mathematics. For
these were not simple verbal tags as names attached to par-
ticular persons and objects are; they were artificial constructs
which behind an innocent façade hid the traces of the par-
ticular kind of logic that went into their making. As Sidney
Hook put it, 'When Aristotle drew up his table of categories
which to him represented the grammar of existence, he was
really projecting the grammar of the Greek language onto the
cosmos.' That grammar has kept us to this day ensnared in its
paradoxes: it made the grandeur and misery of two millennia
of European thought. If Western philosophy, to quote Popper,
consisted of a series of footnotes to Plato, Western science took
a full two thousand years to liberate itself from the hypnotic
effect of Aristotle, whose encyclopedic philosophy penetrated
the very structure of our language. It determined not only
what was 'science' but also what was common sense." [28]

Koestler's point, quite simply, is that the analogies and verbal concepts
we use to explain certain ideas about reality end up affecting our shared
understanding of that reality. Furthermore this affected 'shared understanding' ends up not merely being a private affair but a cultural and
historical heritage that contributes to the foundation upon which future
thinkers build.

Of course there are transcultural exceptions in the worlds of facts and
values. If all information was simply a matter of culture-specific interpretation, then that would invalidate any attempts at 'objective' critical
analysis.

These qualifications not withstanding, let us be quite specific and relate
all this back to one of the main ideas we have discussed so far. How does
something like that affect our understanding of the wonderful gift of God's
son, and furthermore what does all this have to do with Christian art? In
order to answer this we have to go to another writer.

Theologian Cohn Gunton[29] examines two sets of Christological problems that have arisen in the church's thinking. When the early church
fathers were attempting to formulate a Christian defense and a 'Christology' in terms congenial to Greek philosophy, the kinds of problems that
they ran into tended to come from 'above,' meaning that the Incarnation
did not make sense within the world view and framework of philosophical

ideas of these people. How can a mere mortal man, they would ask, subject to change and decay, be a perfect embodiment of the timeless, perfect, Absolute? How can an individual fully express the Eternal Logos and still be fully human?

Questions like that produced a range of different responses, all of them attempting to reconcile the mindboggling concept of the Incarnation with one of the 'official' models of philosophical truth or spiritual reality prevalent at the time. The orthodox theologians of the early church wrestled with the problems of 'two substances in one body'. Some of the heretics on the fringe of the church came up with wilder ideas: solid reality, a kind of first century hologram, a trick of the light. Others made the body of Jesus a 'container' for the mind of God, or they came up with some 'third nature' that was a blended mixture of God and man.

These were some of the responses to the enigma of the Incarnation, as the thinkers worked in the light of the foundational beliefs of the time. The problems came from 'above' caused by the spiritual and philosophical views they already held. The problem is reversed once we enter our own scientific materialistic age. Gunton goes on to point out how in modern secular thinking, the problem is rooted in the questions that come up from 'below.'

God (according to this thinking) has been reduced to a distant mechanical cause, or a vague internalized sense of right and wrong, or has simply been abandoned altogether as an outdated, irrelevant and unworkable hypothesis. How can a dubious label like 'God', they might ask, be meaningfully tied to a solid flesh and blood person in history? Gunton argues that when something as complex and mysterious as the Incarnation is forced through grids of philosophical idealism or rational empirical observation, then some reduction and distortion inevitably occurs.

I have suggested that those 'grids' make their presence felt in the very language we use to try and describe and explore an issue like 'How can Jesus Christ be fully God and fully Man?' Invariably when we are handling something as 'neutral' as language, we don't catch the hidden problems alluded to above, and they in turn impact our exploration and explanation of the mystery of God's wonderful gift to us. Here is Koestler again:

> 'The awkward fact' said L.L. Whyte, 'that reason, as we
> know it, is never aware of its hidden assumptions – has been
> too much for some philosophers and even many scientists to
> admit.' One of the philosophers who saw this clearly was

> *Wittgenstein: 'Propositions cannot represent the logical form:*
> *this mirrors itself in the propositions. That which mirrors*
> *itself in language, language cannot represent. That which*
> *expresses itself in language, we cannot represent.' The preju-*
> *dices and impurities which have become incorporated into*
> *the verbal concepts of a given 'universe of discourse' cannot be*
> *undone by any amount of discourse within the frame of refer-*
> *ence of that universe. The rules of the game, however absurd,*
> *cannot be altered by playing that game. Among all forms of*
> *mentation, verbal thinking is the most articulate, the most*
> *complex, and the most vulnerable to infectious diseases. It*
> *is liable to absorb whispered suggestions, and to incorporate*
> *them as hidden persuaders into the code. Language can be-*
> *come a screen which stands between the thinker and the real-*
> *ity. This is the reason why true creativity often starts where*
> *language ends.*[30]

True creativity often starts where language ends. Of course, as I have suggested, each culture is rooted in a worldview that significantly impacts its expression and language, from its philosophical and scientific talk down to its every day speech. This is why I propose that the arts gift us with a neutral ground, an area of exploration and play, in which we can use our artistic gift to explore the meaning of the wonderful gift of God in His only Son. I want to suggest some of the ways in which art forms can help us get a grasp on some central Christian truths.

Some Christian thinkers, such as Denis De Rougemont have already explored this idea. He writes about the art of painting:

> *'The expression veils what is expressed, while manifest-*
> *ing at the same time to our senses. For what is expressed is*
> *not separable from the means of expression, or is so by abuse*
> *only. What makes manifest is at the same time that which*
> *conceals. The meaning of a picture, for example is not dis-*
> *tinct from the colors, forms, proportions by which, and also*
> *in which it exists. It is possible to see them and not see it. In*
> *the eyes of reason the means remain essentially heterogeneous*
> *to the reality they express. Why those and not others? And yet*
> *we would know nothing of it without them. I do not press the*
> *matter. I am obliged to limit myself to indicating the point of*

*possible departure of a dialectic which would find its model
and perhaps its norm in the doctrine of the second person of
the Trinity, and in a meditation on its mystery."* [31]

If the author is correct, then the gift of art in some way helps us to understand the gifting of God to us in the sending of his son. A painting is at once a combination of its material properties, paint, canvas and so on, and also an expression of a personal vision or idea.

Another author, Aidan Nicholls, takes it further. He points back to the arguments that raged through the early church concerning the use of images and icons. He argues that the materiality and the limitations of the art medium impress rather than obscure the reality of the artistic idea, or in this case the Incarnate God upon the 'faithful' observer. Nicholls proposes a three dimensional understanding of art, an understanding that involves the intention of the artist, the materiality of the medium, and the receptive faith of the observer.[32]

Other writers have appealed to the arts as providing the best models for understanding and appreciating the gift of God's Son. If the limitations and the contingencies of the medium enhance and embody the realities of the message, as De Rougemont and Nicholls suggest, then we might be able to push the analogy further.

Gunton, whom I quoted earlier on the problems of philosophical language and the Incarnation suggests music as providing a more accurate model for our understanding. He talks of two notes in a chord. Perhaps the metaphor could be extended to forms of composition like the fugue, in which two related melodic themes unfold at the same time. Dancer Judith Rock wrote this about the arts providing a metaphor for the Incarnation:

*'An authentic artwork is an indissoluble union of line,
color, movement, sound, rhythm, idea. The oneness of being
that the early Christian writers tried to communicate when
they described Christ, fully human and fully divine, is not
unlike the oneness of form and content achieved in a success-
ful dance, symphony, sculpture, play or novel.'* [33]

Other authors have turned to metaphor, analogy, parable and story-telling in their quest for a deeper understanding of both Biblical materials and theological concepts. If, as we saw with Gunton's arguments, the idea of the Incarnation suffered as it was viewed through the distorting lenses of a particular world view, then it could be, as Hans Frei has argued, that the Bible has often been read through a grid of contemporary interpretive practices that paid no attention to the governing concept of narrative. Not only does a recognition of the role of narrative and the central role of metaphor awaken us to a more sympathetic reading of Scripture in its intended context, but it also gives us another model for understanding the life, work and person of Jesus.[34] Other authors have pursued the idea of narrative beyond biblical materials and concerns into the larger realm of theology and philosophy. Robert Paul Roth, in his work 'The theater of God',[35] pushes forward the category of 'story' as a replacement for all the philosophical metaphors and scientific models that have been used to give 'intellectual shape' to our ideas about God.

Roth, like Gunton and others, recognizes the distorting and limiting effects of our worldview and its language when it comes to talking about God. The arts can provide us with a more flexible vocabulary for the conversation. Perhaps they can also provide us with a bridge between the old world and the new.

The world around us, as we suggested earlier, is undergoing what is referred to as a 'paradigm shift' in which many of the older 'universal' certainties are depicted as being specific to our particular culture and 'socially constructed model of knowledge.'

How these developing insights apply to informing a dynamic Christian presence in this emerging picture of the world is still being sketched out,[36] but I believe that informed and sensitive Christian artists and thinkers have a vital role to play. This role, as I have said, not only involves communication with the world at large, but it also involves providing models of thinking 'with' and 'through' art for those within the church.

8. Towards a Lost Wax Mind

In an earlier chapter we touched on the tensions and conflicts between cultures, those within a culture, and then those within the heart of an individual. We explored those tensions against a backdrop of the 'creative redemption' of a supremely creative God who wants to redeem His creation.

I want to make some concluding observations about art practice and intention using this 'three level' approach as a framework. In order to help us remember what some of the key issues are, and also to find a new way of breaking the issue(s) down into sections for further consideration I want to direct our attention to a passage of Scripture: Hebrews 4:12-15.

Here, everything becomes accountable to a dynamic word of God that can probe into the soul and the spirit. It can separate between bone and marrow. It is able to accurately divide between the thoughts and the intentions of the heart.

I understand that the author of Hebrews drew upon the imagery of a butcher's shop in which sides of flayed meat are hung, in order to provide a metaphor for the analytical and probing insight of the dynamic word of God. Furthermore he drew upon imagery from the wrestling match, in which the victorious opponent has pinned his foe and the foe is paralyzed, vulnerable and exposed. Nothing is hidden from God's sight.

A current way of talking about the dynamic word of God's power might be in pointing to those marvelous 'mysteries of life' images of a weeks old baby in embryo. Or we could point to the way that beams of laser light are used in very delicate surgery. Metaphors like that barely approach the subtlety and power of God's dynamic word in the depths and accuracy of its insight. When we turn our attention back to art making we find three categories the dynamic word of God is able to probe into.

Firstly, the word of God explores and comments upon the relationship between the idea and the art object: the artistic intention and the material expression. It is not enough to have a beautiful idea. As we have discussed in earlier chapters, how the idea is expressed has its own integrity and its own accountability.

We cannot appeal to the brilliance of a concept, or some mystical inspiration in order to justify shoddy art. The Apostle James, in the second chapter of his epistle, challenged his readers about the necessary relationship between their good intentions and practical deeds of mercy.

The dynamic word of God is able to probe into and judge the relationship between an idea and how it is realized as an art object. It assigns appropriate weight and judgment to both aspects of art, without getting the two confused, or using the elevated nature of one to justify the poor execution of the other.

Secondly, the dynamic word of God is able to probe the relationship between form and content. The overall art experience emerges because of the tension between and 'marriage' of form and content. For a truly Christian approach to art, form cannot simply be a secondary thing, or a 'necessary evil' in relation to content. Many of us have unconsciously inherited the idea of a sharp dichotomy between form and content that is rooted more in the philosophical presuppositions of our own culture than any truly biblical revelation. This confused thinking about 'form' and 'content' is sometimes combined with an overall suspicion of the world of creativity and the 'realm of the senses.'

We explored that idea in our chapter on 'yielding our bodies as living sacrifices'. Here, we recognize that the dynamic word of God makes appropriate insight into and judgment of the necessary relationship between form and content when it comes to art making. To surrender content and focus merely on form is to lapse into mere decorationism. However, to insist on the priority of content over form is to betray the content.

The rules governing the construction of a sermon are different from those governing a parable. It is, as we have suggested throughout these chapters, the same with art objects. The artmaker, therefore needs to be sensitive not only to the relationship between an idea and its material expression, but also the relationship between form and content. Earlier, I quoted something from Judith Rock, a Christian dancer living in New York. She spoke of an analogous relationship between the 'oneness of being' the early Christian writers tried to communicate when they described the Incarnation, and the 'oneness' of form and content in a successfully realized work of art. She goes on to say:

> '*The perfection of Christ's union of humanity and divinity was so important to understand that two heresies were like warning signs for those straying too far in either direction. We must remember, the early church fathers warned, that this union is not a confusion of divine and human. But at the same time we must also avoid drawing false distinctions between the divine and the human in Christ. The union of humanity and divinity in the incarnation of Christ, and the union of form and content in a successful artwork, are neither a confusion of unlike elements nor a hard and fast distinction between unlike elements. Both relationships are much more suggestive of a marriage.*' [37]

If the dynamic word of God judges rightly between an inspired idea and the artistic expression of that idea, and also judges rightly between the 'marriage partners' of form and content, then the third category we should explore is the relationship between the art work and our response to it.

Let us take the example of a rock song. To say that I have an idea for a song is not the same as reading you the lyrics. Simply reading the lyric sheet is not the same as listening to the song on the record. There is the melody to consider, as well as the tonal qualities and the volume of the instruments used in performance. There may be studio added enhancements to the 'raw' track. Then there are all the personal associations and memories triggered by the hearing of the song. All these elements play into how we appreciate that particular song.

I think that this idea applies in the larger field of the various arts. I do not believe that art exists in total isolation from its context of being responded to. Similarly, as I have tried to point out in various ways earlier, I do not believe we can approach art or fully understand its impact without being aware of those factors of response, both in terms of our 'gut level' response, and also the 'subtext' to a work created by our awareness of the history of responses to it.

When we use a symbol or an image, or we saturate a canvas with a field of rich color, or fill an empty room with sound, it is to awaken an informed, multilevel response in the hearer and viewer.

When we try and ignore all the issues raised above (idea/ expression, form/ content and artwork/ response) and simply bulldoze our way towards making 'really *Christian* art' in order to 'reach as many people as possible' then we make something less than art, and also we show little respect for the humanity and the God-given 'capacity for response' of our intended audience.

So much for art in our culture. I want finally to briefly summarize some of the earlier concerns about our relationships to other cultures by considering some words from the Apostle Peter. He speaks of living and thinking as 'aliens and strangers' (1 Peter 2: 11-12) in order to appropriately judge our own culture from within, but also to give those in other cultures good reason to praise God.

I have suggested that in order to appreciate the way in which the arts work and find value in different cultures we might have to step back and take a long critical look at our own culture. As I have suggested before, problems occur when we take our own cultural and ethnic standards of what is good, bad, and valid, and make them a basis for universally judging peoples and cultures different to our own.

In the arts for example, we might be prone to think in terms of museums and galleries, and artwork that uses certain kinds of representation or certain kinds of abstraction. This might bias the way in which we read so-called 'primitive' art, and it might prevent our true understanding and appreciation of other approaches to art in ritual, ceremony, symbol and decoration.

If, on the other hand we learn to live as 'aliens and strangers,' we will be able, with the help of the Holy Spirit to come to an understanding of the structures and limitations of a culture like ours, while still living inside it. This is one aspect of 'the crucified mind' that we explored in our chapter about 'the living sacrifice' and the senses. The other aspect of this 'crucified/ aliens and strangers' mindset is the renewed respect and appreciation we will show to all cultures and their arts, not just our own, will create a basis for other people groups to respect us and the good attitudes we display.

I believe that while God extends his grace to us, a truly 'Christian' culture is a culture that exhibits the best of human creativity, redeemed and transformed by the living Christ. I believe that it will be diverse in its expression. We can listen to black gospel music or the Indonesian gamelan music of the Protestant church of Bali. We can look at Dutch landscape painting or beautiful Indian miniatures. We can sit enthralled by a medieval mystery play, or a traditional Javanese shadowplay. We can watch graceful ballet or the use of traditional dance forms to the glory of God. All this diversity and plurality is an expression of the many-sided wisdom of God.

As we think through the potentialities offered to us in the idea of cultural diversity, and the problems presented to us by the relationship between cultural form and spiritual root, I want to give one final metaphor that I believe will help us apply the lessons from Hebrews 4 and elsewhere to the current issue. This metaphor was generated in discussion during the closing sessions of the arts conference in Bali in 1989. We can call it 'lost wax thinking' or 'wax and gold' thinking.

An image is made of wax. Clay is packed round it and allowed to harden into a mold. The mold is heated, the wax melts, and it runs out of a small hole in the bottom of the mold. Molten metal is poured into a small opening at the top of the mold. As it moves through the hardened clay it cleans out the residue of the wax and fills the space left by the molten wax. The metal cools and hardens. Eventually the clay mold is broken. A metal or golden image remains.

If the wax image can be taken to represent a traditional spiritual impulse, around which the 'clay' of human expression and cultural form is packed, and if we can assume that these powers were defeated, disarmed and taken captive through the cross (Colossians 1: 15-22 and elsewhere) then simply pouring Christ into the mold of a particular cultural form should of necessity melt and burn out the traditional impulse behind the cultural expression and reappropriate the expression to Christ's glory.

I think that when we think through the implications of our own art practices in light of 'dynamic Word' thinking of Hebrews 4, and then think in terms of art and communication across cultures in the light of Peter's 'aliens and strangers' thinking and also our model of 'lost wax' thinking, we can draw three conclusions. In the light of how this book opened, I think it is appropriate to consider these conclusions under the image of 'gifts.'

We as artists are given three gifts. Firstly, we as art makers and thinkers receive the gift of a larger place in which to make art. The artist is set free from the quest to make 'timeless' or universally applicable art on one hand as he or she deals within a localized, concrete context.

We are also set free from the commodity-oriented rat race, because the artwork is designed not so much to compete in the marketplace, or reach the lowest common denominator, as to somehow both embody and communicate the gift of God's love in a way that honors the humanity and the responsiveness of the observer/ participant.

Secondly, we receive the gift of an enriched and broadened worldview. The artmaker is no longer boxed in by his or her own culturally specific ideas when it comes to understanding the world. We have suggested in earlier chapters how such culturally specific worldviews evolve, and how they limit our knowledge of both creation and the Creator. Now, with this gift, the picture is more rounded, complete.

Thirdly, we are given the gift of appreciation for a diversity of cultural expression and creative endeavor. As we have suggested, one aspect of 'aliens and strangers/ crucified mind' listening and looking is learning how not to impose culturally specific but unconsciously universalized standards of artistic value upon the work done in other cultures.

Once we have learned not to dismiss work that does not quite 'measure up' to the values that we have inherited, or conversely, project a set of alien 'meanings' onto someone's work that say more about our cultural biases than the real intention of the artmaker, we will be free to truly appreciate the many different approaches to art evidenced among the peoples of other cultures.

9. Only a Beginning

This obviously is only the beginning of an exploration into a very complex set of issues. We have only just begun to map out some possible connections between a variety of fields of inquiry that to my mind are related, but traditionally are kept in separate compartments. A more substantial investigation of those connections, with an application of the findings to our understanding of art, will take a much larger book.

I am very grateful to Louis and Mary Neely, pastors of Warehouse Ministries for their long-standing vision concerning the use of the arts for the glory of God. They, and the church as a whole, have provided (and continue to provide) much ongoing encouragement and very generous support as I continue to think through and work out some of these issues. Thanks also to David and Susan Fetcho of Bay Area Christian Artists Network and New Performance Consort for their friendship, ongoing discussions, and ground level participation in untangling some of these ideas.

PART TWO:
Scratching the Surface

10. The Light By Which We See

`He who would be head must also be the bridge' Ancient Welsh proverb

`And this field wherein now we are, may be an instance: for you see by the ancient ridges or lands, though now overgrowne with bushes, it hath been arable land, and now become fit for no use, unless it be reformed.'
-The Surveieors dialogue 1610

As I think about what interested me in art and creativity in the first place, I am taken back to some of the memories of my early childhood in Walthamstow, East London. One of the first toys I can remember getting was a kaleidoscope, and even now I can recall how I would stare down the tube at the complex radiating patterns the carefully placed mirrors would create out of the clusters of loose colored beads.

I can also recall walking daily through Saint Mary's Churchyard to get to `infants' school'. One afternoon, on my way home, I and some friends came across a grown up doing a painting of Saint Mary's Church. I was fascinated by the evident concentration of the painter as he added touches of color to the small canvas.

I remember that my mother and I would visit the William Morris museum in Forest Road. We would spend hours looking at the drawings and designs for wallpaper and stained glass that Morris and those like him in the Arts and Crafts movement hoped would help build a bridge between art and life. Such a bridge was necessary, Morris and others argued, because some of the technological innovations and standardization in manufacturing goods was leading to a loss of quality in production of those goods.

They also contributed to an aesthetic 'dumbing down' of a society already caught up in the euphoria of progress and profits before all else. For Morris, the fight against such erosion became an increasingly political one. He would later describe his ideals of such an integrated 'arts and crafts' vision in tones of disillusionment and despair. His bleak analysis of the driving forces of the industrial revolution, the resulting economic expansion and the corresponding patterns of society saw little room for anything other than outright dismissal of his concerns, or worse, the relentless co optation and assimilation of any attempt to introduce anything genuinely creative and humanizing into the culture of the time.

If Morris, and others such as mentor figure John Ruskin were appalled by the demoralizing and dehumanizing effects of the 'culture' of the time, they would be even more so today. A global digital dimension has supplemented the poisonous factory chimneys and the rivers flowing with industrial waste. Latter day social and cultural theorists such as Guy Debord and Jean Baudrillard argue that the essentially alienating and dehumanizing aspects of modern society have passed from the realm of product, even the realm of dominant theory, into the realm of the all embracing 'image.'

For these latter day theorists, there is no way out. This is scant encouragement for those apologists, theologians and pastors who feel compelled to critique the demoralizing effects of today's pop culture. It is even more discouraging for those of us who want to think about a 'Christian approach' not just to critiquing images but actually making them. As is often the case, one of the surest ways forward involves first going back to basics.

Colin Gunton begins his paper 'Creation and Re-creation: an Exploration of some themes in Aesthetics and Theology' by reminding us that the dominant theories about art and beauty in our culture have been worked out in the shadow of the Greek Philosophers like Plato rather than the light of the Psalms. Many of our theories, even recent ones, about 'the beautiful' 'the sublime' and the realm of the aesthetic have been built upon developments, variations, and sometimes reactions to these ancient Philosophers' assertions about the ideal realm of 'pure eternal forms' or mathematical perfection and the correspondingly inferior and secondary status of material reality and human history.

Some of these ancient thinkers accordingly, saw poets and artists as mere dabblers in this inferior realm, or a corrupting influence in society. Their imperfect copies of an imperfect copy merely deceived, or lead astray. At the very best, their work might be useful as a reminder of ultimate concerns. In this view, the artisan imposes shapely `form' upon shapeless matter, and the result might be a serviceable stepping stone or ladder rung up to this loftier, ideal `realm' of eternal forms or a sequence of musical notes was intended to remind you that there was an unheard, sublime, mathematically proportioned `music of the spheres.'

Others, such as Aristotle, had a somewhat more congenial understanding of art. Aristotle is popularly understood as arguing for an essential reality of and in the world, rather than above in the ideal forms. He argued for .the arts, not merely as stepping stones, but also, in the case of poetry and drama, as medicinal mirrors that offered `catharsis,' purification for those who truly looked into them. The audience who witnessed negative emotions dramatized might, in the act of watching and reflecting on what they see, be purged of those emotions. In this argument, there was something curative and therapeutic at work. Tragedy was good for the soul.

In both these cases, the arts as ladder to the absolute, or purifying mirror for the soul, there were some shared basic assumptions about material reality. Matter was rehabilitated, restrained by the imposition of `form' and harnessed to some social or moral purpose.. Versions of these arguments about essences, materials and purposes in art making have continued with us in various forms, even casting their shadow, understandably enough, over some of the arguments about art and the Christian faith. However, the first step out of this shadow has less to do with hunting down scattered biblical references to art and artisans, and more to do with reflecting on what the biblical writers have to say about creation and its relationship to and with the creator.

The Psalmists use a number of potent metaphors to describe the created order responding to God and reflecting His Glory. The writers talk of a sky that `inscribes' and declares God's majesty, and a landscape that `gushes' praise to its creator (Psalm 19: 1-3) The psalmist goes on to suggest that there are traces or echoes of this dynamic created order woven deep into the roots of human culture and language. Elsewhere, the Old Testament writers paint glowing pictures of nature's response to God's particular covenantal dealings with Israel (Hosea 2:21-23, Isaiah 44:21, 55:12)

If we can be inspired and instructed by these writers' vibrant use of language, and think in the light of a genuinely biblical understanding of the value of the created order, we can see material reality is not made of inert or perverse substances or merely a footnote to a realm of beautiful ideas. It positively explodes into complexity of form and pattern in its response to its maker. Accordingly, we can think of `form,' not as some sort of necessary straitjacket on `delinquent' matter, but more as a dancing partner caught up in a whirling dance that both celebrates and reflects the glory of God.

We have briefly touched on the responsive and reflective relationship between the created orders and their creator. Can this throw some light on how we proceed to think about the creative word and the actual form the creation takes? Is it permissible to see the patterns of form and matter in `nature' as a consequence of God's `Creative Word,' something like a fractal pattern? Do the patterns unfold as a result of the creative word of God? Or are they unfolding in response to the presence of God? The language of Scripture suggests both.

Also, according to Scripture all things `hold together' in the dynamic embrace of the Creative and sustaining Word .(Hebrews 1:3) Think of the patterns resulting from the activity of metal filings on a piece of paper when a magnet is held beneath the paper. The patterns both emerge and are held in place because of that magnet. Think of the patterns in a kaleidoscope. What seems to be a jumble of colored fragments is suddenly transformed by three or more reflective surfaces into a rich and complex visual order.

Accordingly, we can view `The Word' as generating patterns, or as the `hidden' dynamic holding all things together, or as an ordering context into which events freely unfold. Admittedly, all these are metaphors. As such they cast, at best, a faint light. They will, however, barely scratch the surface of what Paul hints at in his epistle to the Colossians when he speaks of all things being created in, through , and for Christ.(Col 1:15-20) Nor should we lose sight of Paul's words to the Corinthians about the `dark glass' we look through when we are looking into things of this magnitude.(1 Cor 13:11-12)

With these qualifications in mind I return to our earlier metaphor of the dance. Paul writes to the believers in Rome about the visible orders reflecting something of the invisible characteristics of God. (Rom 1:20) Perhaps the dynamic of the celebratory and reflective dance of the material orders faintly echoes something of the movement of the members of the Godhead themselves. The early church fathers spoke of the way in which the members of the Trinity indwelt one another, and were distinguished and defined, not only in their own actions, but also in the dynamic act of deferentially affirming one another. The term they used was `Circumsessio' in the Latin, and in the Greek it was Perichoresis. Perichoresis means, literally, to `dance around.'

To summarize, we can view the Creative word as generating the forms, containing them, and binding them together.. We can view the dynamic interactions of form and matter, or of all the complex levels of the created order as distantly analogous to some of the `invisible qualities' of the Triune God . In all this, our view will be necessarily limited and provisional. Somewhat like that small, half-finished painting of St Mary's Church in Walthamstow. Nonetheless these tentative metaphorical explorations will have served their purpose if they have moved us and our understanding of beauty, order and creation out of the deadly shadows of Plato's cave and into the light of some genuine categories of thought with a corresponding vocabulary for our discussion about art, life, creation and the purposes of God.

Paul writes of these purposes of God elsewhere (Romans 8:19-27) and speaks of a created order `groaning' in anticipation of the consummation of God's plans. Paul writes of us groaning also, and then of the Holy Spirit praying in us and for us with groans and sighs too deep for our understanding. Perhaps, here, we can look at this tension between anticipation and consummation, creation and recreation as a drama. However, we are not innocent bystanders, or passive observers. This drama enfolds us all. If there is a cathartic element to *this* drama, it will have little to do with the subjective response of an audience.

Colin Gunton goes on in his paper on aesthetics to suggest that alternate readings of the notion of `catharsis' relocate it in the structure of art form itself. The tension and ultimate resolution in the work's surface, or the dramatic passage *is* the cathartic element. For us, then, the concept will be rooted and grounded in the way in which God empathetically identifies and `suffers with' His fallen and damaged creation and expresses and communicates that empathic identification. The ultimate catharsis in the drama of creation and recreation is in how the broken heart of God finds formal expression in the content of Jesus's ministry.

Elsewhere, the Apostle writes of the implications of this for the church. He writes to the Ephesians of how the Many-sided Wisdom of God' is revealed and reflected in the purified reconciled community of believers(Eph 3:10) Paul's terms in the Greek are suggestive of both the many sparkling faces of a diamond, and also the variety of color and form in a bed of flowers. And while these images are beautiful, it surely should be that the creative expressions of those called into fellowship with such a purified, reconciled community will be even more beautiful.

Of course the groans of desire to see some kind of bridge built between nature, culture and spirit represent a deep human longing, that has expressed itself in a variety of ways in the history of world cultures. For the ancient philosopher, as we have seen, natural form and cultural artifact were stepping-stones to the ideal. For some more recent thinkers and artists, this 'ideal' was internalized as a primary category of what it means to be human, a way of meaningfully ordering our experience of the world, or a way of empathetically linking imagination and nature. For those like William Morris art making and cultural work were intended to be liberating and humanizing elements in a just society.

But today, as I indicated earlier, all these paradigms, and their social and cultural implications are in question. In fact, the very possibility of a governing paradigm or 'metanarrative' is in doubt. Numerous thinkers, from the ancient Skeptics to the modern deconstructors have set about relativizing and dismantling the different philosophical, scientific, cultural and even linguistic foundations of our concepts of Truth and Reality….arguing that truth concepts are inextricably linked to the exercise of power, and arguing that it is futile to even talk about 'reality' in a society completely addicted to 'the spectacle.'

They suggest that, far from having any arguable 'absolutes' in the moral, spiritual or aesthetic realms, all we have are culturally relative 'truths', historically constructed versions of 'reality', and socially determined 'values'. While the vulnerability and the circularity of these 'deconstructive' lines of argument have long been rehearsed, I believe there is a way of using the partial truth of these insights in a way that not only redeems the human cry for meaning, but also returns us to our confessional roots.

Firstly, we must remember Paul's words to the Corinthians about the factors inhibiting our clear vision and complete knowledge.. Secondly, we should recall the light the biblical writers shed on such ideas as historical construction and social determination.

The historicity of the resurrection of Christ must have some bearing upon any discussions about 'constructions of reality' -- historical or otherwise. Or else, as Paul says we have no basis for a coherent discussion of our faith, let alone anything else like art, truth and beauty. (1 Cor 15:12-19)

Indeed, our values and ideas may be socially determined, but need this be the acquisitive, alienated kind of social structure that drove William Morris at first to despair, and then into Revolutionary Socialism? We have already alluded to an alternative, a 'purified, reconciled community' in Ephesus. Was not this same congregation the original recipients of

John's gospel, in which Jesus asks that the fellowship of the `perichoretic community' of Father son and Spirit be opened out to the community of believers (John 17)? Jesus prays and invites us into the heart of God. He further asks us to explore, unfold and demonstrate our redeemed and renewed personhood in community with others He has extended that invitation to.

This renewed, relational understanding of our personhood should also open our eyes of faith to the co-inherent, perichoretic dimensions of the rest of creation. As the 17th Century mystic Thomas Traherne suggests, our `right seeing' of the visible world will be dependent upon our grasp of the depth of God's love for us. And this, as much as anything else we have touched on so far will have an impact on our ideas of art, beauty and truth.

With the `redemption' of those partial insights in place, and the all too human cry for meaning and liberation still echoing I want to offer one more suggestion concerning beauty and truth.   And this one speaks of a biological constant beneath the historical and cultural relativities. Because our God is not merely a beautiful idea that sprang up unbidden in Plato's cave, but rather underwent human birth as a kicking, screaming infant in a stable, we are bound to reject those attempts to `redeem' art and beauty from the world of materials and appearances.

It may well be, as the British Art critic the late Peter Fuller, and more recently cultural anthropologist Ellen Disanayake has argued, that many of our notions of beauty, significant form and aesthetic delight are rooted among our earliest memories as an infant, during that time when our emerging sense of `self' in relation to `world' drew upon both biological and social experience. This, at least, is a shared experience impervious to critical deconstruction, and possibly the origin of much of our talk of `significant form' and `aesthetic disinterest'. As such, this experience is no less part of the created order that God redeems, and no less part of the `visible order' that echoes the `invisible things' of the Godhead. This is the very heartbeat of our imaginative wonder, our aesthetic delight, and our hunger for right relationships and justice.

Coda: The Only Dance There Is?

When I was in Russia in early 1992 I visited the famed Hermitage museum in Saint Petersburg and spent some time looking at Matisse's radiant painting `The Dancers'. This painting with its flatly colored flesh toned forms cavorting in a circular dance against brilliant fields of green and blue, has been cited by John Lane as emblematic and illustrative of the `dance' at the center of reality as described by different modern thinkers... Reality accoriding to these thinkers , at its heart, is most readily observed in the relationship between things, whether we are discussing the ecosystem or quantum physics. Some theorists look for corresponding analogies in different forms of Eastern Mysticism. Thomas F. Torrance replies to these assertions by pointing out that the concept of the Trinity and the idea of `perichoresis' speaks directly to the issue of the `ontorelational' notion of reality, and grounds it within Christian confession. Mattisse's image celebrates the primary dance at the heart of the created order. This dance, in turn, points beyond itself to God.

Hanging on my office wall is one of the souvenirs from that trip: a reproduction of a 16th century Icon of the Trinity by Andrei Rubliev. Douglas Adams exegetes this painting, reminding us how the distortions of perspective, the suggested forms, the facial expressions and bodily gestures of `Abraham's three visitors'. Even the subtle dynamics of the color choices and placement, all sweep the eye from figure to figure in a circular movement that is suggestive of the movement of the Trinity itself.

The deep hunger for art that speaks to human conditions and needs from a faith perspective was surely evidenced recently in the tremendous public response to the `Seeing salvation' show at the National Gallery in London. This collection of Christ centered imagery, drawn from the canons of Western `High Art' drew crowds that responded in ways that had little to do with mere appreciation of purely `aesthetic' concerns or conversely any skeptical deconstruction of the controlling and constraining agendas of the museum in relation to public taste. There was a deeply human response to something that slipped past those categories.

And finally, when I was in China, a year and a half ago at the International Festival of the Arts I saw a cultural spectacle that somehow summed up all the concerns touched on in these remarks, and found expression in very contemporary terms while remaining true to its faith perspective. Handel's Messiah, although to be performed by an orchestra made up of Western and Chinese musicians, was still feared by government officals as 'largely incomprehensible' and therefore potentially boring for its intended Chinese audience. Accordingly they inquired about the possibility of projected subtitles. Therefore , during the actual performance, neon subtitles were on prominent display.

The composer's text, a veritable tapestry of Scripture references to Christ and his work flashed and winked in neon Chinese characters as the audience sat and listened to the accompanying music. I cannot speak for how this affected the rest of the audience. I can only speak for what occurred to me. In some ways, it resembled a mixed media 'post modern' event, in which media and signs circulate with no final resting place, no fixed meaning. In other ways it was very different. The dance of sights, signs and sounds, far from celebrating the absence of any meaning, seemed, to me, decisively, and perhaps, given the context, subversively to celebrate the presence of the author of all meaning.

All our attempts to talk about art and creativity from a Christian perspective often seems as effective and relevant as the act of lighting candles in broad daylight. Nonetheless I suggested that we try and think about art less in the shadow of the dominant theories about beauty and truth and more in the light of Colin Gunton's insightful remarks about the aesthetics of creation and recreation. I further suggested that we might benefit from looking at some of these issues in the light of various scriptures, ranging from the Psalms to the epistles of the apostle Paul, and Jesus' 'high priestly prayer' in the Gospel of John.

I closed by suggesting that some of our responses to beauty and order might be grounded in our bodily experience, and our childhood memories. These things too are part of the created order that God has redeemed. However, when all is said and done, I have to confess that my own hunger for a bridge between art and life drives me back to my recollections of walking through a church yard on the way to school, and my memories of the complex, radiant patterns in a child's kaleidoscope.

Key Works Drawn Upon Throughout Article

1. 'Creation and Recreation: An Exploration of Some Themes in Aesthetics and Theology' Colin Gunton, *Modern Theology*, no.2, pp.1-19.

2. The Fractal Geometry of Nature' Benoit Mandelbrot *W H Freeman and company* 1982

3. 'Theoria: Art and the absence of Grace' Peter Fuller. *Chatto and Windus*. London UK 1988. Fuller ends his book length study of Ruskin and his circle of influence, by suggesting some links between Ruskin's aesthetics, his

`Natural Theology' and the work and ideas of Benoit Mandelbrot.

4. `Art and Psychoanalysis' and `The Naked Artist: Art and Biology' Peter Fuller, *Writers and Readers Co-operative Publishing* 1980 and 1983 respectively.

5. Art and Intimacy: How the Arts Began' Ellen Dissanayake. *University of Washington Press* 2000

6. The Seamless web' by Stanley Burnshaw *George Brazillier* 1970

7. `Philosophy in The Flesh: The Embodied Mind and its Challenge to Western Thought' George Lakoff and Mark Johnson *Basic Books* 1999. This book suggests that all our philosophical theories and speculations, however abstract, can be traced to metaphors based in our bodily experience of the world.

8. `The Living Tree: Art and the Sacred' John Lane. *Green Books* UK 198

9. The Ground and Grammar of Theology (James W. Richard Lectures, University of Virginia.) Thomas F Torrance, Belfast: *Christian Journals Ltd.* 1980,

5. The Knight's Move: The Relational Logic of the Spirit in Theology and Science' James E Loder and W. Jim Neidhardt. Helmers House pub 1992

6. `Transcendence with The Human body in Art' Doug Adams. Crossroad 1991

11. Crossing the Boundaries

`God does not weave a loose web' --Hilda Doolittle

When I had volunteered my services as a poetry teacher for my daughter's second grade class, I and the kids worked extensively together on poems about nature, animals, feelings and memories. We ended a series of classes by having a discussion on the importance of poetry...and to get the discussion going I handed out copies of a poem by Robert Bridges that mentioned over seventy different kinds of English wildflower (and the poem rhymed!) I then asked everyone to imagine what it would be like if a third of the flower types the poet mentioned no longer existed. Further, the only evidence that they had existed was contained in this poem. Would that make a poem like this an important one? What about art and poetry in general...in terms of 'real life' on our planet? This, for me, was one factor influencing my desire to work on the mixed media collaboration `Crossing the Boundaries' with visual artist Gaylen Stewart.

Gaylen Stewart is an Ohio-based painter and mixed media artist who has been building a reputation through numerous solo shows and group exhibits over the years. Our paths crossed regularly from the early 90s on at places like Cornerstone Festival where he would be exhibiting work, doing seminars and offering workshops and critiques for the `Artrageous' section of the festival. On the last day of the 1996 festival we began to discuss working together on a collaboration, and possibly pursuing a grant to that end. Gaylen followed up on this and the Ohio arts council did very generously make a grant towards this project.

When Gaylen and I began to make initial plans for this collaboration, in the summer of 1996, we wanted the working process and resulting installation to some ways echo the natural systems we were drawing our imagery from. Not only the working process and resulting installation drew influence from these systems, but also the different extensions of the work, including talks, lectures and descriptive articles like this one are influenced in this way. While the show was installed at Gallery W in Sacramento, we held some Sunday school classes in the gallery, and I interacted with the children about the ideas, images and sounds.

We generated three metaphors for mapping the development of the work. Under the heading of 'seeds' I talked about how Gaylen worked as an artist and how I worked as a writer/composer, and what ideas came up as we began to discuss this collaboration project. Under the heading of 'Cross pollination' (or 1-4 grade equivalent) we discussed our working method together and how we communicated back and forth as the art work progressed.. Under the heading of 'layers' we discussed how Gaylen builds up layers of images in paint, collage, words and printed images on his canvasses, and I talked about how the poetry and music was put together and combined. We also saw how the resulting installation, as well as individual works had many layers to it.

I have found that keeping metaphors like this in mind is helpful in explaining Gaylen's art and our collaboration to different groups of people.. Gaylen combines images, text, paint, mechanically reproduced images, collaged petals, wings and light boxes in what amounts to a ' confessional assemblage' that narrates his ongoing concern with nature, science, spirituality and art. The work is at once rich, evocative, multilayered, and allusive both to personal issues, as well as larger concerns involving art and 'Nature.' When I look at Gaylen's work I think of three interactive layers. Each layer represents a different concern.

Gaylen literally brings 'the real world' into his art by collaging plants, leaves, grass and dead butterflies onto his canvasses. However, he is not only concerned with direct allusion to natural processes, he is also concerned with redemptive imagery and metaphors. For Gaylen aspects of the natural world, butterflies and honeycombs etc become metaphors for spiritual truths and processes. So both the material 'stuff' element, and the symbolic 'referent' element make their way into Gaylen's work.

Thirdly, Gaylen is not only concerned with the material and the metaphor. He is also concerned with the personal, confessional, autobiographical aspects of image making. Gaylen's own 'personal confession' of healing from cancer and allusions to his own spiritual growth are worked into the surfaces, both in choice of imagery and also in the collaging in of 'material elements' such as X-rays.

Over the past ten years I had been writing and publishing small chapbooks of poetry and prose based on my travels in India, South East Asia and Europe. I also began to perform and record some of the poetry over a background of sound textures and musical loops.. Not only was I interested in exploring the possibilities of extending work through different varieties of print and recorded media, but I was also intent on exploring and learning from those cultures where art, life and spirituality were integrated in ways that seemed very different to some of our approaches to art in the West.

I was to discover, however, that in our own tradition poets and thinkers such as William Wordsworth and John Ruskin, understood the need for an integrated, humanizing approach to art and culture. They also understood that such an approach needed to be rooted , not only in a sensitivity towards the natural world, but also towards the spiritual one.

Accordingly, Gaylen and I approached our collaboration `Crossing the Boundaries' mindful of the similarities in our working methods. We also shared the concern that our method of working together would somehow echo and reflect elements of our chosen subject.

As Gaylen began to draw upon his own resources for natural symbols and images, I began to manipulate textbook and encyclopedia entries on plant systems, animal migratory patterns and environmental concerns. I would fold and cut together some of these texts allowing the resulting word patterns and turns of phrase to form a seedbed of ideas for the poems. I would send Gaylen photocopies of manipulated text, drafts of poems and plant images copied from old textbooks, and Gaylen, in turn, would reproduce these words and images on his canvas, integrating them into the developing multilayered surfaces of his work. On one occasion he sent me photographs of several paintings in progress, and I was able to integrate my response to his images into a poem. As the poem was being written, I tried to bring our working method to bear upon the way the music was put together, sending Gaylen rough mixes of works in progress so that he could listen as he painted.

Once the poems were finished I recorded them over a background of shifting sound textures, composed of orchestral sound loops and recordings of birdsong I had made one late fall morning with my daughters..... These sections of birdsong had been edited, looped, layered , and in some cases slowed down. The resulting sound patterns were woven through the orchestral and synthesizer sequences. Most of these sequences carried fragments and echoes of a 'root' melodic pattern, sketched out in different voices and different tempos.

We did this with computer programming, and also by mixing the completed tracks down in such a way that elements of other tracks could be heard 'soaking through' in the background. This , for me, continued the themes of layering, process and pattern, that informed the poetry and the paintings. It added continuity to the album of poetry and music when listened to, in sequence, as a whole.

Further, it brought a sense of harmony to the overall installation which featured seven CD players, all playing different tracks at once. These CD players were installed among the fifteen paintings and they held the gallery visitor in an all embracing gentle web of sounds and words. The overall sound would slowly change as the viewer moved from painting to painting. Again, the installation experience not only alluded in some ways to our method of collaboration, but also reflected aspects of nature itself.

This show has been circulating for about a year, showing in a variety of gallery and museum settings throughout the USA. However, it is com- ing to the end of its 'life' as an installation experience. Parts of it will live on, in a variety of secondary forms. Many have walked away with their own compact disc, to listen to the tracks in sequence and contemplate the accompanying booklet of color reproductions of Gaylen's images. Many have visited Gaylen's website www.gaylen.com to read about the work, the artists, and to look again at the reproduced images.

Gallery talks, slide lectures and descriptive articles like this one con- tinue to link people back to both aspects of the artwork and some of the ideas and concerns behind it. However, once the original installation has run its exhibition course all that we will have left are these myriad second- ary forms, all referring back to an 'original ' that no longer exists. These secondary forms, of course, have their own 'identity' and also contribute something of their own to shaping of these different expressions.

When in Cambridge, England last year to participate in the C S Lewis centenary conference I was able to read one of the poems with its backing track, and show some slides of Gaylen's paintings. All this took place in an old Anglican Church where the sounds echoed richly off the wooden pews, and Gaylen's slides, their colors somewhat muted by the encroach- ing daylight, looked like faded ancient tapestries, surrounded by radiant stained glass windows and ornate brass fittings.

That weaving together of imagery and sounds from 'nature' with the highly wrought symbolic expressions of faith not only reminds me of some of the potential and promise I glimpsed in cultures like the Balinese one. It also reminds me that the Christian worldview was an important element in the theories and practice of poets like William Wordsworth and art theorists like John Ruskin.

If their concerns for maintaining the vital links between faith, nature and culture were important in the early years of the 19th Century, how much more important are these concerns at the beginning of the 21st? Questions like these bring me full circle to that class room of children I began this piece with. It was there that we discussed the value and place of art and creativity in a world where a single poem might end up serving as a kind of epitaph for an entire species of flower.

12. Fear and Multicultural Trembling

*'He finds in every work of art, in every part of the world,
a trace of that heavenly spark which went out from Him,
through the breast of man, into man's own lesser creations,
from which it sends its gleams back to the great Creator. The
Gothic is as pleasing to Him as the Greek temple, and to
Him the rough war chant of savages sounds as sweet as the
art of choral and church song....'*
    *-Outpourings From the Heart of an Art Loving Friar'
1797.*

Perhaps we can see some truth in these words on `Universality, Tolerance and the Love of Mankind in Art' penned for artists by Wilhelm Wackenroder (1773-1798.) On a good day, our creative work, regardless of our ethnocultural background, glorifies God, either as a conscious offering back to Him, or as a light onto our constructed, creative nature.

We would also acknowledge Wackenroder's prescient insights into how we use our own culture(s) as a yardstick for measuring the culture(s) of our neighbor, near and far. He might have found much to ponder in the recent debates about `Multiculturalism' in the arts. I certainly did as I stared up into the night sky of Sanur, Bali in the spring of 2002.

There were many more stars than I was used to seeing, scattered across the sky. I began to wonder how one would navigate in the light of so many stars. I also reminded myself that the light I was seeing came from stars long since burned out.

When sharing this during a devotional at a Traditional Media Unit international arts conference in Chiang Mai, Thailand in November I focused on some verses from Paul's letter to the Philippians, specifically the ones that described the Philippian believers as shining like stars in the sky as they held out the Word of Life (Phil 2:15.)

I was looking out at over sixty art makers and media workers from literally all over the world, gathered together in this conference room. They represented diverse backgrounds and diverse artistic disciplines and practices. For me, they, too, shone like stars in the sky just as Paul had described the Philippians. Accordingly I drew upon my experience in Sanur, Bali to talk about many stars, complex navigation, and the long reach of starlight.

This conference in Northern Thailand was one of our TMU gatherings of international artists and media workers. We had been coming together in places like Bali and Eastern Europe over the last fourteen years to celebrate the culturally diverse forms of Christian creative expression. At this conference, we explored Filipino dance styles, Chinese landscape painting, popular music from Malawi and traditional folk theater from Thailand.

We exhibited artwork, watched video and shot it, danced, sang and sat in silence. We considered everything from native craft traditions through to modern and postmodern art theories, all in the light of the Kingdom of God. As always, this diversity of practice and approaches was deeply rooted in biblical reflection on and worship of our Creator Father God, who judges, redeems and recreates.

I wish Wackenroder could have been with us. But what would he make of the 21st Century? As I reminded our conference participants in Thailand, most Christians and therefore, most Christian artists live and work in what is called 'The Majority World' The many different ideas about art that they bring to the table are important considerations for us all if we want to remain part of the conversation about art and faith in the 21st Century. Wackenroder might agree with this observation, but how would he handle some of the other aspects of the 21st century?

Many diverse threads of communication and culture have been woven together by the digital communications revolution. Many in the global village have witnessed 'The death of distance' thanks to the computer and the satellite. These are not the only factors reshaping our world.

Secularism, perhaps not dead, is seen as a mixed blessing by those caught between their desire for progress and their need to cling fiercely to tradition. National identity, ethnic pride and cultural origins have been brought back into the conversation...sometimes in alarming ways.

The church has recently witnessed a redemptive counterpart to this. There is a growing 'First Peoples' movement in which Tribes, clans and people groups express their Christian faith more in the light of their cultural heritage, and less in the shadow of the European missionary. I reminded my friends in Thailand that the church is also witness to a rebirth of interest in the arts. Some are drawn to 'media rich' ancient liturgies, others seek multimedia stepping-stones into today's post-literate society. There would be a growing need for creative thinkers and makers.

In the light of what I shared I believe that we all have to carefully sift through our ideas about 'multiculturalism.' Multiculturalism is a phrase that was linked to the arguments of 1980s and '90s that (some say) paralyzed any discussion of artistic value by reducing all positions to politics and preferences. According to some, you were blindfolded by privilege and prejudice when it came to judging the creative work of those marginalized by the dominant (First World?) culture.

Opponents of this point of view did not want to see discussions about quality and value in culture held prisoner by political correctness. They felt that this approach bled art dry of its essential qualities and inevitably did a disservice to its makers, regardless of where they came from. Still others were wary of our faddish interest in putting other cultures on display, because the work invariably was seen as a footnote to our evolutionary theories of cultural and social progress, or as a confirmation of our theories about the 'universal language' of art, regardless of the artwork's original context.

Does this fundamentally 20th century argument have any place in 21st Century reality? To be sure, our habits of seeing will reveal cultural bias, and accordingly affect our preferences and values. How do we balance our critical awareness of this with our appreciation of what we find good in art? Perhaps we can start by digging into the multicultural/cross cultural soil buried deep in our own backyard.

Hayum's reconstruction of the original context and reception of Grunewald's Isenheim altarpiece places it as a vital visual component in the administration of the Eucharist in an Antonite monastery/hospital setting. Hayum's scholarly exploration of medical conditions, optical theories, and church history only deepens and enriches our understanding of this work.

C S Lewis wrote of a 'discarded image' when describing for us the very different worldview and cosmology of the society 'behind' the turning pages of medieval and renaissance literature. For most of us, our open Bible call us into a world very alien to our own, and yet one we need to grasp more deeply if we are to grow in and communicate our faith.

The Isenheim altarpiece, of course, is not only relevant to the poor sufferers of `St Anthony's fire' in a sixteenth century hospice. It speaks as art, and as a paradigm of empathic contextually sensitive communication to us today.

Lewis allows that not everyone will want a medieval text illuminated by an explanation of the world behind it. Some readers will just want to read the text. Further, I would never limit the significance and the imperatives woven through the famous `mind of Christ' section in Phil 2 :5-11 to the actual situation in Philippi Paul was addressing. It speaks to us here and now.

The light from this passage, and others, reaches us like starlight, a great distance from its source and origin but still useful for navigation today…if we know how to navigate. Thankfully, the tools for such a task, both in print, and now online are widely available. The computer not only networks the global village, but it also contributes to a virtual `new Reformation'. Many tools for Bible study are now online or now available in software packages .

I believe the computer can in some ways assist a new revolution or reformation of our ideas, just as the printing press aided the reformation in the 16th century. I believe that many of us now can go a long way towards nailing down the correct meaning and the significance of a passage of Scripture. I believe that as we do this, our eyes will open to the missional, and multicultural dimensions of Scripture.

The Bible as a whole is shaped by a missional imperative . It has always been God's purpose, some contend, for God's glory to be reflected not merely in the diverse intricacies of nature, but also refracted through the languages and the cultural expressions of the peoples, tribes and nations. The fact that this God-honoring cultural diversity finds a hollow echo in the relativistic `multiculturalism' of Eurocentric `Postmodernism' is no reason to abandon it. With the tools now available to many of us for giving the revealed Word of God its proper due, we now have even less excuse for avoiding the issue..

The New Testament writers heralded a day of a truly multicultural response to God (in keeping with the Old Testament prophets see Is 2: 3-5, Zech 8: 20, John 4: 23, Acts 2: 1-4) They accordingly took a balanced approach to their own `cultures' and that of their neighbors. Paul used his cross-cultural awareness to strategic advantage. He quoted Greek poets in Acts 17, and outlined `the advantages' of Hebrew culture in Romans 3.

What Paul and the others argued against was not cultural distinction, but the attempts to use such distinctions as a basis of bargaining with God (as in the keeping of the Jewish Law or claiming that Abraham was your father) or as a means of cultivating a sense of social superiority over others, be they barbarians, women, slaves and so on (See Gal 3: 28, see also Romans 11: 19-21 concerning `Gentile' arrogance). Jesus's own `High Priestly' prayer recorded in John 17 spoke of His present and future followers being `one,' not because they had been assimilated into a particular social and cultural tradition, but because they had been drawn into fellowship with the Trinue God.

I suggest this not only because the apparent confusion over these issues promotes a diluted reading of Scripture, and a correspondingly distorted Gospel. I suggest it also because those who are genuinely different from us, and yet none the less just as redeemed, can only enrich our discussions about beauty and excellence in the arts.

Paul's prayer for the Ephesians makes mention of coming to a knowledge of the Love of God `together with all the saints' (Eph 3: 18) and in the same chapter he writes of a reconciled community of faith revealing the many sided or faceted wisdom of God. Paul's imagery in the original Greek suggests both the varieties found in a flowerbed and the different faces of a precious stone.(Eph 3: 10) A God-honoring collective cultural expression will be defined by the way it `makes room' for the genuinely different. This definition will be the fingerprint  and heartbeat of `The Community of the Beautiful.

And yet, as I said in Chiang Mai, we need to pursue excellence and quality in our artistic endeavors. The art making that takes place in the 21st century multicultural church will be informed by the different conversations that surround that concept. (Hebrews 10: 24-25)

We must also look for ways of learning from one another about how art and life connect in different cultures. Public funding and museum space might be an issue in one culture. A village setting and a harvest might be an issue in another.

Are there ways of giving `voice' to the multicultural reality of the 21st century church in the arts, honoring excellence and diversity, and recognizing the strategic opportunities the many bridges between art and life afford in most of the world? Artwork made by Christians from Africa, the Americas, Eastern Europe and Asia is now reaching us by old and new media. But what about us? Have we moved beyond 20th century arguments into 21st century reality? And how will we interact with that reality in the clear guiding light of Scripture?

In 1998, at a British conference celebrating the life and work of C. S. Lewis I met painter/ mixed media artist Rick Harden. Rick was dreaming of seeing his experiences in Kosovo, Bosnia and elsewhere translated into a mixed media installation that would open doors of reconciliation and hope in these troubled areas. Now, five years later, this installation 'A field of Poppies' is touring through the Balkans.

When the show opened in Prishtina the director of the Kosovo art gallery spoke eloquently of the work's potential role in helping bridge the spiritual gulfs between the Balkan nations. Further, the Kosova minister of culture has proposed that the work be permanently installed in a `Peace Museum' in Kosovo.

Rick's mixed media installation combines painting, drawing, video, sound, and computer scans of his own drawings combined with children's artwork form these troubled areas. It is not only recognized as wonderful, cutting edge art, it is also seen by its hosting community as a site for reflection, and a seedbed for dreams of reconciliation.

A year later, I was in the Philippines as guest of artists Mark and Robin Merrill (Robin co- chaired the Multicultural panel at the last CIVA conference.) The artwork they sold not only funded the other forms of ministry they were involved in to street kids, former prostitutes and AIDS patients, it also opened the door to gallery openings and panel discussion participation. This gave them credibility in presenting a 'Kingdom' per-spective on burning issues in the Filipino public arena.

I was in the Philippines en route to the People's Republic of China. I was going to participate in an arts festival organized by `International Festival of the Arts' and Colin Harbinson. When Colin Harbinson, au-thor of Toymaker and Son, realized that the arts were the heartbeat of a people, or nation, he also realized that the strategy of `cultural exchange' would open many doors in a Nation 'in transition.' Accordingly he began to organize arts conferences under the umbrella of `International Festival of the Arts'.

A wide array of artists from all over the world would enter this nation, always at the invitation of the hosting community and share in a festival of cultural exchange. This was always with a view to sharing not only ar-tistic diversity and excellence, but also working towards a number of other appropriately restorative relationships centered in the felt and expressed needs of the hosting community.. Art, life, peoples and cultures were re-demptively connected and deeply enriched.

No doubt there are other examples and there is still room for more of us at the table, if we choose to contribute.. If we choose not to, cit-ing the faddishness or political machinations of earlier discussions about 'multiculturalism' then, in my opinion we are doomed to increasing ir-relevance. I believe a time is coming, and in fact, now is, when what is termed 'contemporary Christian art' or art made by Christians' will be authentically so, only to the extent that it is grounded in a recognition of the multicultural reality of the 21ˢᵗ century.

> *"Therefore, my dear friends, as you have always obeyed—not only in my presence, but now much more in my absence—continue to work out your salvation with fear and trembling, for it is God who works in you to will and to act according to his good purpose." –Phillipians 2: 12, 13.*

13. When Worlds Collide: The Novels of Shusaku Endo

I recently had the privilege of hearing Japanese author Shusaku Endo lecture in Berkeley. I have read him avidly since first discovering his work two years ago while living in England. Many questions surfaced for me as I read through material on Endo and listened to him speak.

What do you make of a man who says that once he is writing a novel he makes no judgment on the lives and actions of his characters? What do you make of a man who believes that "the eyes of Christ" are on his characters, and who writes conscious of that loving gaze upon the people he has turned loose in his fiction?

Endo has been a prolific writer. His work includes drama, fiction, and nonfiction historical and biographical studies. He is popular and respected in Japan. His work, in spite of its variety of textures and surfaces, is rooted in a specific set of concerns. Since he began to write, Endo has looked for ways of presenting Christianity that are appropriate for his culture. He draws on his own experiences and his own unanswered questions in order to inform and energize his fiction.

Endo has frequently described his childhood baptism into the Catholic church, and the influences of his subsequent questions and doubts on his work. His university studies centered on the writings of French Catholic novelists like Francois Mauriac. He spent some time in Europe in further study, but ill health forced his return to Japan and required an extensive hospitalization.

Endo's observations on his own Catholicism, and the examples of French writers he studied, combined powerfully with his observations of a nominally Christian West and his experiences of hospital procedure in his homeland. These provided the groundwork for the themes and images that surface through the body of his written work. Endo observed that Europe had departed from an all but nominal Christian confession. Nonetheless, many of the Christian ideas about the individual, morality, and accountability were still powerful influences in that culture.

Endo sought in some of his work to depict a Japan that had no such sensibilities, that approached the moral and ethical problems involved, say, in conducting experiments on American prisoners of war (in the novel *The Sea and Poison*) purely and simply in terms of expediency. Endo made his point in a different way by focusing novels such as *Volcano* on lapsed Catholic westerners who seek complete assimilation into Japanese culture by throwing off their past. They find themselves still being nagged by residual notions of guilt and accountability from their western Christian upbringing.

But it is not merely guilt and a sense of moral violation that haunts Endo's characters. Guilt's counterpart, the forgiving and self-sacrificing love of Christ, haunts the lives of some of Endo's simple villagers who, although they publicly declare their renunciation of the Christian faith under threat of torture, nonetheless cling to the belief that Christ sees them in the extremity of their situation and forgives them. (Several of Endo's works focus on a period of Japanese history when an attempt was made to stamp out the Christian faith.) In Endo's works the characters cleave in faith to this almost motherly, forgiving aspect of Jesus; the Catholic priests wrestle with the implication of a forgiving Christ as they themselves are threatened with the torture of their converts or themselves in an attempt to get them to apostasize.

Endo's characters, both eastern and western, are haunted by a specific Christ—a paternal. Judicial figure in the West and a maternal, forgiving figure in the East. In this haunting they bear some resemblance to the "fundamentalists" of Flannery O'Connor's fiction. Endo has repeatedly registered his conviction that a gospel centered on the forgiving, nurturing Christ is far more appropriate for his homeland than the stern, judgmental model imported from the West.

It is my intention through this somewhat brief exploration of some of Endo's work to get at the root of his concern. I want to focus specifically on three major books: *Silence*, a novel that was deemed problematic and controversial when it appeared in the '60s; *Wonderful Fool*, an earlier novel that under the guise of a comedy of social observation grants us insight into the kind of Christ figure most appropriate to the situation of contemporary Japan (published in the late '50s), and the more recent *The Samurai*, which advances Endo's concerns in a more convincing and balanced way. Not only is *Samurai's* theology of contexts and cultures more developed but it works better as fiction (although that may rest to some extent with the translators of Endo's work).

Endo is put forward as being one of the more accessible of the Japanese novelists. Nonetheless his work may read strangely to westerners. What reading I've done in Asian theories about art reveals an emphasis on understatement, allusion, juxtaposition, and a montage of images that proceed more along symbolic lines than on clearly defined sequential or obviously narrative ones. The work comes to its fruition only through the sympathetic participation of its audience. The carefully placed images. References, and delicate fragments are gathered together and slowly worked into a whole under an empathic and contemplative reading or listening from its audience.

It may be that Endo's work, moving within some clearly defined cultural and historical conventions, awakens in us aspects of empathy and creative receptivity that have lain somewhat dormant or have been massaged into inactivity by the increasingly superficial narrative conventions of our own popular media. It may also be that the very unfamiliarity of the storytelling conventions in Japanese fiction work critically for us, gently urging us toward a critical reappraisal of our own dominant assumptions of naturalist or realist fiction— in short—whatever we think it takes to tell a "good story." This is my testimony from reading Shusaku Endo and his novels. Perhaps it will be yours too.

Endo, in both his work and his many interviews, uses powerful images to describe the problems of faith and doubt in Japan as he sees them. He points out that he has tried in his work to fashion a Christian faith that fits more like a familiar Japanese kimono than the ill—fitting western suit he received as a child. Endo has also coined the term "mudswamp" to describe a Japan of moral torpor and lukewarmness in sharp contrast to the western and Christian specifics of the individual: doubt, faith, action, and consequences. The mudswamp meets such notions of consequence and accountability with the dreamy fatalism of karma. It meets the specificity of a Messiah with a diffusion of spiritual energies throughout the realm of nature.

Some feel that the mudswamp wins in Endo's powerful and problematic novel Silence. The book focuses largely on the attempts of the Japanese persecutors and their ally, an older apostate priest, to coerce the Japanese believers to abandon their new—found Christianity. Many of the arguments against a vital Christianity being able to take root in Japan surface in the dialogues between a younger priest, Rodriguez, and the older lapsed priest, Feirrera. Rodriguez comes to Japan freshly enthused with the task of reaching souls for Christ. It is in his lengthy dialogue with the older apostasized priest, Feirrera, that many of the issues Endo has referred to begin to surface. The older priest now works with the authorities in their efforts to undermine the work of the missionaries and to force the converts into renouncing the faith.

Rather than focus on the heroism of the martyrs, Endo dwells in his fiction within the souls and hearts of those priests and converts who wrestle with their doubt and confusion against the backdrop of the utterly alien Asian mindset and culture and also within the boundaries of their weakness, fear, and humanity. Endo has remarked that he himself would not be able to endure the tortures that some of these priests were threatened with and so he chose not to try and write of those who did.

A number of issues surface in the dialogues between the priests and their persecutors. Japan is considered as unreceptive to the gospel not because of any overt hostility but because of its mentality that seems to absorb everything without being affected by it. This mentality is depicted as being one in which life, death, the individual, and the other elements of nature are simply aspects of a larger all-embracing continuity linked to a cyclical view of time. Such a perspective cuts the ground from under any discussion of sin and individual accountability. It also suggests that any conversions to Christianity will be superficial and short—lived, resting on a reinterpretation of Christian language that preserves the form but radically alters the substance in accordance with the dominant world view.

To make his point the older priest uses the image of a butterfly caught in a spider's web. The form remains caught there while its substance slowly rots away. This mudswamp world view not only robs the Christian faith of any potential moral consequence by rendering the notions of God, sin, and death meaningless terms in a completely alien world view, but also changes the meaning and intention of the Christian vocabulary in such a way that it renders all conversions highly suspect.

The persecuting authorities go to lengths to assure those they are persecuting that they regard the formal act of renouncing Christ as unreal as the conversions. They urge the captured priests to step onto a sort of Oriental ikon, as a mere formality. This notion of formality haunts Endo's later work, specifically in *The Samurai*. Traveling Japanese merchants enroute to

Spain consider the trading advantages that might be theirs if they submit to the formality of Christian baptism.

In order to torment the priests further, the lives of some of the Japanese converts, even those who have formally renounced the faith, are placed in the balance of the priest's decision. The authorities and their allies, the apostasized priests like Feirrera, use everything from sophisticated reasoning, moral blackmail, and the threat of the extreme torture of "the pit" in order to persuade the active priests to renounce their faith and to cease from proselytizing. The torture known as "the pit" consisted of suspending the priest upside down in a large pit full of filth and refuse. A small cut would be made to allow a slow letting of blood and the priest would be left hung in this way, with one hand untied so that he could signal a decision to recant. If the priest refused to do this he would be left to die slowly. This took days, in some cases as much as a week, if not longer.

The authorities in the novel *Silence* and the companion play, *The Golden Country*, use everything from sophisticated forms of reasoning to threats of torture and death in order to persuade these priests to give up their Christian faith. Insofar as Endo's novels focus more on the priests who give in and apostasize rather than on the obvious heroism of the Christian marytrs, it seems worth asking if Christ is at work here. I believe that Endo is arguing for a Christ who is present with these priests in the midst of their weakness and failure. It would be hard to establish such an argument on the basis of a book like *Silence* alone; but I believe that an overview of Endo's translated works leads us in the direction of a sympathetic and compassionate Christ who sides with the weak, the unfortunate, and the unloved.

And where better to begin than with a naively ambitious and enthusiastic priest who has been pitched headfirst into a strange foreign culture and has been assured that all the work he has attempted to do is of no real value, that his prized "conversions" rest on a few elementary semantic misunderstandings, and that many of his former converts—even those who have formally renounced their new faith—will die unless he publicly severs his allegiance with Christianity.

Endo confronts his character with all this and with the threat of torture, and then gives him an experience of an inner voice that the frightened and confused priest assumes to be that of Christ. The voice urges the priest to step on the image of Christ—that is, to apostatize. Endo, in his historical works such as *Silence*, establishes some contrasts between the dreamy blurred boundaries of the Japanese world view and the clear-cut and often arrogant motivations and energies of his Catholic priests who loudly proclaim the universality of their gospel. Sometimes the holy ambition of these priests is sullied by political considerations. Sometimes the conversions the Japanese merchants undergo are merely for the trading advantages that might follow.

In the midst of this, Endo's Christ is a mysterious and controversial figure. In *Silence* the Catholic priest is confronted with the collapse of everything he held true. Under the threat of torture he hears a voice urging him to step on the image of Christ. The voice claims to be that of Christ himself. Is this really Jesus showing a radical compassion for the priest in his vulnerability and frightened humanity, or is it the Japanese mudswamp taking on another guise in an attempt to tempt the priest away from the cost of his vocation? Endo leaves such questions unanswered in *Silence* and *The Golden Country*. Both points of view have been argued by Endo's critics and translators.

Wonderful Fool gives us some insight into the kind of Jesus Endo feels is most congenial and available to the Japanese mind. If Endo's historical novels pitch a clearly defined Christianity against the Japanese mindset, then in a work like *Wonderful Fool* the emphasis shifts. Here the figure from the West is not an aggressive domineering Catholic priest intent on evangelizing the heathen, but a lumbering and absurdly sentimental failed seminary student. And the contrasting East is no longer some vague psychic landscape in which plants, animals, humans, and local spirit beings are all merely tributaries flowing to and from a primary oneness, but a polite modern society of materialistic values and impeccable social manners. The resulting cultural collision is as extreme as in Endo's historical novels, but throws a little more light.

In *Fool*, the failed seminarian who has come to stay with a Japanese family works as a Christ figure as he tries, often comically, to empathize with the outcast and the unloved— much to the embarrassment of his hosts. Endo's large-hearted character embarks on a series of misadventures that involve stray dogs, prostitutes, and gangsters. The Jesus we see at work in this and other Endo books evades formal categorization without evaporating into mysticism. Endo's Christ-figures find their homes in their whole—hearted identification with the weak, suffering, and unloved.

Critics of Endo's earlier works, such as *Silence*, have asked why his books are so popular if Japan indeed is so unreceptive to things Christian. Also the options allowed in a book like *Silence* seem controversial and potentially heretical. Endo has never pretended to be a theologian. I believe that the apparently problematic aspects of some of his fiction serve us well in the complex issues it asks readers to confront. The recent novel *Samurai* represents a significant advance for Endo, not necessarily because he has unduly tamed the more problematic aspects of his fictional inquiries into the heart of Christianity, but because he has found a balanced way of accommodating them within a complex of subplots that serve the full humanity of the characters depicted, the strengths and weaknesses of their various cultures, and how all of that plays on their responses to the gospel. Endo's fiction is satisfying because it does not avoid or simplify the hard issues.

Samurai traces the attempts of Velasco, a wily and ambitious Franciscan, to secure exclusive rights for his mission organization to proselytize in Japan. In exchange he offers to mediate in the establishing of a favorable trading situation between the Japanese and the Spanish. He takes some Samurai with him on a voyage to Spain—among them the warrior Hasekura, who at first is disdainful and indifferent toward the "weak man on a cross" who seems to haunt the interests and concerns of those around him. The Japanese merchants Velasco takes with him are in their own way self— seeking and ambitious, evidenced by their willingness to undergo the formality of Christian baptism in order to endear themselves to potential customers.

Velasco of course intends to point to these conversions as trophies and evidence of the success of his missionary society in winning the Japanese. At several points in the novel we eavesdrop on Velasco's prayers to God. At one point he wrestles with the transparent formality of the merchants' baptism. He pleads that the spiritual power latent in the sacrament of baptism will somehow override the superficiality of the decision these men have made.

The little group travels to Spain intent on seeing the king of Spain and to seek an audience with the pope. Hasekura, the samurai, observing the expedient baptism of his fellow travelers, deepens in his contempt for Christ. On their journeys the group runs into another Japanese who had at one time accompanied a missionary in his work among the Indians but has now chosen to live among the Indians, having formally denounced his Christianity. He talks of a Christ who would have made his home among the poor and dispossessed like the Indians. It is only as the party returns to Japan, their mission a failure, that the samurai begins to understand and appreciate this weak and foolish man on a cross whom everyone calls a king. The party returns to renewed hostility toward Christianity in Japan, and the samurai finds himself alone and friendless, stripped of family and culture, and propelled toward an uncertain fate, thanks to his earlier sub-mission to a baptism of expediency.

The samurai's slow journey— from the marshland and his own inter-nalized warrior codes, through strange countries with their own mytholo-gies of power personified in kings and a pope, toward accepting a weak and crucified Christ—is a powerful blend of the inner and the outer. It is a journey at once psychic and geographical in its intent. It is every bit as radical as Velasco's own journey away from his self—centered ambition and into the true meaning of his priestly vocation.

There has been much talk by critics who mistakenly praise this book as merely an historical novel. There has been less talk about the undue focus lavished on the samurai's conversion. Velasco's conversion is every bit as radical and central to this book's resolution. Endo is not in my opinion finally allowing the western-style Christian his due. Velasco converts as profoundly as the samurai does.

In spite of (or perhaps because of) the complexity of the issues at work in Endo's novels, the author has been at pains to point out that he is a novelist, a writer of fiction, rather than a theologian. Although Endo's novels stand at some distance from what we would regard as an academic or a systematic theology, some concerns in Endo's fiction overlap with some recent trends in theology.

For example, some thinkers in the '70s began pointing to storytelling and narrative as more fitting vehicles for theological truth than more tra-ditional systematic methods of theological expression. Advocates point to everything from the parables of Jesus to developments in modern fiction as examples of what they mean. While it would certainly impoverish any reading of Endo's work to suggest that it is merely a body of theological premises dressed up in a storytelling disguise, I believe we can learn about Christ and the expressions of his compassion in cultures quite different from our own. We can also learn not only the power of storytelling to carry messages into the heart but also some lessons about ourselves and the limits in the way we often try to convey truth to others.

These insights, of course, are not limited to the novels of Shusaku Endo. Writers and thinkers dealing in the subject of evangelism and mis-sions have been searching for ways of relating the gospel that are mean-ingful to third-world and nonwestern cultures. Phrases like "redemptive analogies" and "dynamic equivalences" surface in the writings of some of these thinkers, demonstrating their intention toward the people they are trying to reach.

I believe we will gain by turning our attention to the way in which aspects of Endo's fiction resonate with some of the developments in Asian theology. Kosuke Koyama is known for a number of books that take on the problem of a gospel in context from an Asian point of view. His work cries out for a theology in context, thought through from the roots up. He calls out for a water-buffalo theology. He pleads for a God who will acquaint himself with the context of the rural Asian farmer who will "walk at the pace of a waterbuffalo" in the same way that he walked for 40 years in the wilderness with Israelites as they wandered and learned what was in their hearts. Koyama implies that such a God is not only more relevant to the Asian situation, but is in fact more biblical.

Koyama is trying to sensitize us to two nonbiblical models of God at work in history. Both models attempt to trap God inside a historical perspective of specifically cultural origins. One distorted image is the result of the western emphasis on immediacy and instantaneous results, rooted perhaps in a confusion of the efficiency of God's sovereign grace and the efficiency of modern technology. That confusion militates against a God who slows himself down to the pace of the daily life of a rice farmer, or a God who is inefficient enough literally to be stopped dead by the untimely intervention of a Roman cross.

The other unbiblical model of God-at-work-in-time that Koyama attacks is the ahistorical view of time and space in some eastern thought that would simply leave God as a spiritual but contingent being caught in the cycle of death and rebirth. Koyama pinpoints both views as a hindrance to presenting a truly biblical message in an Asian culture. Endo would say that that second model is what informs the threefold insensitivity to God, sin, and death that he attributes to the Japanese mudswamp mentality.

In order to find a model that will help root the gospel in a Japanese context, Koyama goes back to the work of one of his former teachers, Professor Kitamori, author of The Theology of the Pain of God. Koyama draws two principles from the work of his professor with the hopes of picturing a forgiving, loving, and self-sacrificing God in a specifically Asian culture.

The two ideas brought together are tsusumu, a word that means to enfold and enwrap, and tsurasa, a term drawn from the tragic Japanese theater that means to feel inward pain on behalf of others. When these ideas are brought into conjunction, an image can be pictured of the servant of the Lord embracing and enfolding the conflict between God and his people, taking it into his own heart and enduring its pain without fully revealing the extent of his suffering. Kitamori works from this foundation to his concept of love rooted in the pain of God. Koyama draws upon that concept and explores its potential relevance for the contextualization of the gospel in Asia.

While these problems are thought of as missiological and in the realm of a theology in context, nonetheless they also provide some of the themes explored in Endo's fiction. We can be thankful that they do not simply appear as partially digested lumps of theology, but are fully integrated into the imagery and plot unfolding under Endo's hands. In his novels, mud-swamp Japan threatened to take the Christian God, change his name, and chain him to an endless cycle of death and rebirth. Endo's "wonderful fool" somehow combines a clumsiness and awkwardness with a painful sensitivity to the plight of the unlovely and the unlovable. And it is the suffering God who enfolds the struggling priests, even at their weakest moment as they contemplate giving it all up.

While explorers of narrative theologies and missiological problems in the West set about analytically deconstructing the parables or continue to pursue cross-cultural "dynamic equivalences," another Asian theologian, C. S. Song, has published a collection of traditional stories, taken from cultures all over the world, and then explored the meaning of each story for contemporary missionary thought and practice.

In the title story, "Tell Us Our Names," a young bride finds that she is not allowed to serve a meal to her new relatives until she has replied correctly to the riddle, "Tell us our names." Once she has learned the names of the people she is trying to serve, she is allowed to serve them. They take the meal she has prepared for them. Song's plea is simply for a deeper recognition of the complexity and values resident in the cultures that the missionary comes into.

It is wrong, in Song's opinion, to proceed with a gospel couched largely in terms of the missionary's culture and to have that missionary confuse the gospel's universality with the validity of its current form of expression. It is unwise to proceed from there into a patronizing and condescending attitude toward the culture the missionary hopes to speak to. Worse still is to subject the culture to a superficial reading and then to ground much of the resultant theologizing in a subtext of elementary misunderstandings and ethnocentric arrogance.

Song's insights, as well as those of Koyama, find their echoes in the fiction of Shusaku Endo, who struggles in his work to articulate the Christian possibility in the context of a culture that has no sustained Christian history. Perhaps the fight to declare a Christianity without the foundational support of a Christian "history" is, as Endo himself has remarked, "a Cross placed by God upon the shoulders of Japan." Shusaku Endo's work not only helps us to discover a fresh Christ, washed clean of centuries of western myth and our own expectations, but also takes us on an excursion into the heart of the fiction—making process. We should be grateful.

PART THREE:
Work in Progress

14. Emotional Tourist: An Interview with Steve Scott

by Gord Wilson.

GW: Should we start the Steve Scott story in 1970?

SS: I did my foundation course in Essex at Lighton College of further Education then I was at Croyden College of Art from 1971 to 1975. I did three years in the fine arts program, and then did an extra year in film and mixed media, animation, things like that.

GW: At some point there was, shall we say, a collision of worlds, yourself being influenced by some form of evangelical churchmanship, which almost nobody would connect to this sort of an arts interest.

SS: The whole thing kind of happened at once. When I was in high school, I and some friends went to an evangelical Christian outreach. It was a coffee bar, where they give you coffee and you sit down and listen to a gospel group. Like a coffee house, but I think it met in a church hall or something. I started to get involved with a small evangelical free church from that point on. I would say I became a Christian from that point on.

GW: Would you say you were "saved"? or is that just some slang term for this?

SS: That's the point in time I would date my conscious conversion to the Christian faith from. It was the late 'sixties and I was stepping into two subcultures. The evangelical church subculture, and the art school alternative counterculture of the time.

GW: Do I not see echoes of that in all your songs?

SS: I'm sure the tension between those two worlds is there. One, whatever one inherits when one starts going to a local church and declaring oneself to be part of that particular process or movement, and two, in the mid to late 'sixties stepping into the stream of art school culture, and everything that was blossoming around then, which was moving from pop culture and mods and rockers, pop art, very early happenings, into full-blown alternative culture, flower power, psychedelia, Pink Floyd, seeing the Who and Jimi Hendrix play, going and seeing the Mothers of Invention. I kind of stepped onto two elevators at once, as it were, one foot on each.

GW: But no one really would think they're going the same place. I'm playing devil's advocate here, and it's a particularly stupid devil. But the stupid devil would say, you can't be part of all these happenings because they're all about being nude and rolling about in bags and having sex with everything that moves. And you're stuck in this evangelical backwater, so why did Steve manage to do something no one else can do? We find out hundreds of years later that Marshall McLuhan, the media critic of the age, was a Catholic, but the reason we find it out hundreds of years later is because he made a line where nothing Catholic was ever allowed to intrude into his professional life. For some reason, Steve doesn't have that line.

SS: Well, I avoided the stereotypical behaviors associated with that alternative culture. I was, as an evangelical Christian, talking to people about my faith and getting into all kinds of arguments about that. I found myself having different kinds of arguments depending on the subculture I was 'in' at the time. On one hand, there would be arguments about Christianity and whatever variation of crypto or neo Marxism was doing the rounds that week, or Christianity versus some drug- induced revelation. On the other hand, I'd go to a prayer meeting, and ten minutes before I might be noodling around on the piano, and I might use a few black notes along with the white notes, and someone might come up and make a quiet remark about "music offered to strange gods."

However, looking back at that time, I would say that a generation or so later, with labels like 'the post evangelical' and the 'emerging church' that an increasing number of people are understanding that cultural disengagement and irrelevance are not things to be proud of, or to be regarded as a higher spiritual plane.

GW: That pretty much explains the state of television, doesn't it? It's like it is because there's no one in it making it some other way.

SS: It's one thing to avoid doing certain things because you don't want to get trapped by them. It's one thing to be part of a community that intends to help you avoid doing those things because you don't want to be trapped by them. But when insularity becomes your badge, when it becomes, "Jesus Christ, Him crucified, and the way we do things here," then not only have you diluted and distorted the gospel, you've also created a market for all those disaffected, post-denominational, post-evangelical, post-born again, emerging, liquid, ancient-future--you name it, because one can trace these issues in the church all the way back to the 1960s.

I'd say we're two or three generations deep now of people who've attempted to engage with some kind of evangelical truth, been put off by the adjunct culture, and attempted to find some way of moving around the culture and redescribing the truth in a way that makes sense to them and their friends. The other thing I've noticed is that every time something emerges, give it six months and it will end up sanitized and spun for the marketplace. Like what is referred to as Contemporary Christian Music or alt. Christian rock. It sounds like real music that's been fed through something.

GW: Of course, if you listen to alt radio these days, it seems like that too.

SS: Yes, there's a kind of wallpaper flavor to just about everything. Even though some of the patterning on the wallpaper stands out or stood out at some point, when you get stations that run from the '80s through to what's currently being played, you hear bands that tailor their sound, without a hint of irony, and try to capture a particular demographic.

GW: The legend goes that somehow you show up at St. Mark's in the Bowery, in New York, with a plastic bag full of poems. Is that just a made up legend?

SS: When I came to visit America in 1976, I contacted the guy who was running the readings at St. Mark's in the Bowery. (I think his name was Ed Freidman) to discuss a possiblilty of a reading, and he scheduled me with someone else later that summer. I was in New York at the beginning of the summer, then I was on the west coast for a while and I hit New York on the way back out and did a Monday night reading. I'd just had a little book called Ghost Dance come out, which was published in England, and was sort of a collage poem.

When I was in America I had a 16mm print of Ghost Dance with me, which I screened here and there. It's a collage film with some 16mm footage off the TV screen, I bought some old reels of standard 8mm film and we projected that and I filmed some of that back, intercutting TV footage, the negatives along with the original and also the black and white cutting copy which was kind of inferior and grainy, and coming up with a hybrid collage film. I'd gotten a composite print of that whole thing made and I was screening that. The book was an attempt to do in print what I'd done with the film. So I did a few readings in England and in America with that.

As I say, I'd seen a number of films made this way, collage films, reedited found footage etc and I wanted to do some work in this way. After I got back from America, the next thing I did was put together a four screen film project called Correspondences, that was part of something called the Expanded Cinema festival at the Institute of Contemporary Art in London. That was a week long event with everyone from established filmmakers, sculptors, other people doing artistic things with film, multi-projection events, right down to student types such as myself who managed to squeeze a slot in there somewhere. Correspondences was some footage I had shot and edited into four reels. With four projectors going, you created a kind of collage film poem in which different sections mirrored each other, or corresponded in some way with what else was being projected.

Then I came back to America in 1977 because while I was at Croydon School of Art I met Randy Stonehill who introduced me to Larry Norman who liked some of my songs. While I was out for a visit in 1976, we'd talked about the possibility of doing a record. So I came back in 1977 and we began to do preliminary work on an album that was to be called Moving Pictures. People working on it were Tom Howard and Mark Heard and Randy Stonehill and Jon Linn and other luminaries. The album got close to being finished but a variety of things happened with myself and with Solid Rock, Norman's record company, and stuff. And I ended up moving to Sacramento and getting involved with Warehouse Christian Ministries principally because they expressed great interest in the arts.

I began to pursue the idea of thinking about art and making art in Sacramento, along with the idea of talking about art and thinking about where we were going as artists. There was obviously room for ongoing reflection and conversation around these issues. Twenty five plus years on there still is. I drew upon what I'd seen at Nigel Goodwin's Arts Centre group, what I'd heard from people like Hans Rookmaaker, and the like. I desired to take the best of what I'd heard there, the best of what I'd seen done by artists in England in the 'seventies: film maker Norman Stone, Poet/Rock journalist Steve Turner, bands like the Technos and After the Fire. In my opinion there was an awful lot of promising stuff going on in terms of both popular culture and artistic practice in that first generation (that I was aware of) of Christian thinkers and artists who were coming out of L'Abri and the influence of Francis Schaeffer and the Arts Centre group.

Last time I checked, I think Peter Banks of After the Fire was living in Walthamstow which is where I was born. Rupert Loydell is the cousin of Beverly Sage, the wife of the late, lamented Steve Fairnie. Bev was in a singing trio called Soul Truth (then based in the coastal town of Torquay), and in that singing trio was a woman named Judy who ended up marrying Andy Piercy of After the Fire. I first ran into them at an event which I think was a Youth for Christ thing, (Youth week 69 or 70) at which the young Nigel Goodwin spoke, as well as the Reverend Canon Harry Sutton. Goodwin was the founding figurehead of the Arts Centre group in London, who put out the magazine, Cut. This was 1970. The young Andy Piercy was there, the young Steve Fairnie was there. Fiarnie and the other Steve (Rowles) formed a band called Fish Co., and then The Technos (full name Techno Twins).Bev was part of that too.

Andy was part of or was becoming part of a folk duo called Ishmael and Andy. I think after Andy went on to After the Fire, Ishmael had a couple of bands: Ishmael United, a sort of punk rock outfit, and then Rev Counta and the Speedoze. The afore mentioned Nigel Goodwin was just starting the Arts Centre group in Kensington. Shortly after that Youth Week, Goodwin was leading a group of art students through the Richard Hamilton show at the Tate gallery. I ended up tagging along. Richard Hamilton was identified with the UK end of the pop art scene, along with people like Peter Blake, who did the Sgt Pepper sleeve. Hamilton did that famous painting of Mick Jagger in handcuffs.

But a lot of the stuff I had been exposed to in my own sort of art school/ counterculture/ poetry reading meanderings had given me a broader exposure at a primary level to what was going on in the 'sixties and in the arts. I thought, there's got to be more to how we engage with the culture. It's not just about what Rookmaaker and Schaeffer are talking about. I saw Rookmaaker lecture at the Royal College of Art in 1973. The feeling I got was that he would be the last one to assume that he represented any sort of closure on the conversation. People like him always struck me as being in process and open to discussion and understanding that this was just the beginning of something. Unfortunately, some of the conversations I had with some of the people who came up around them had more of an oversimplified sense of closure, and an "insider/ outsider" approach to things.

If you've had any kind of exposure to the mindset that goes with certain aspects of the evangelical church there's this kind of closure and shutting down that occurs. Traditionally it occurs when they start talking about Andrew Murray or Watchman Nee or the Keswick Convention or some sort of deeper or higher life experience. Some kind of demarcation, like that's it. A kind of badge, a secret handshake, a magic decoder ring, the 'in' crowd etc. with a corresponding reduced view of everything. When you encounter that in the context of the pietistic tradition of the evangelical subculture, that's one thing.

But I encountered the same sort of apathy toward what was happening on the fringes of the artistic community. It was all reductively filtered through what people thought they understood of Schaeffer and Rookmaaker-- sort of "ok, we've got it, this is how it is." I was just seeing too much real art, and so I thought, no, it's not as simple as that." On the other hand, to be fair, Goodwin and Rookmaaker never came off like, "ok, we've got it," but rather their approach was, "this is the beginning of a conversation and we're in this for the long haul."

And there was huge cultural change going on. If I wanted to sum it up in a nutshell, what I was getting a whiff of when I was hanging out in the art world or the art scene per se, as sort of a hanger on or fringe observer, was the culture that would later be described by some as "post-modernism." This culture was emerging through the late 'sixties into the 'seventies. The underlying theory began to show up in large chunks towards the end of the 'seventies. All those kinds of scepticisms about the nature of truth, about politics, about cultural dominance, about the relation of language to reality, about science's description of reality, all those were part of the brew, and were part of what was influencing artistic practice.

The thing that I felt about the modes of analysis being attributed to Francis Schaeffer and Hans Rookmaaker was that when they were talking about art, they were talking about modernism as a cul de sac, as a philosophical statement, but this was as modernism was being eclipsed by postmodernism. I thought, that's all well and good, but we're all post-modern now. What do you have to say about that?

To be fair, Rookmaker was not alone in doing `art as a window onto a larger set of social concerns'. John Berger's Ways of Seeing was out about then. I'm aware that there is Marxist analysis and other kinds of left of center social analysis of what was happening in culture, that did not idealize culture, but saw it embedded in a particular social and historical matrix. I look at someone like Rookmaaker like, "ok, we've got the Marxist one, maybe the Frankfurt School one, and here's one that comes out of a Dutch Reformed approach to things." If I were to imagine a bookshelf, I would put Rookmaaker next to John Berger, Albert Hauser, Raymond Williams or any of those guys who are attempting to do a large scale diagnostic and locate art or artistic practice or artistic result as symptomatic, whether they're arguing from the political right or left, or whatever.

In another sense, I can see Rookmaaker well in place for what was going on as the attempt to come up with a particular kind of Christian position in a European culture say, in Amsterdam. Working under the influence of people like Abraham Kuyper, coming out with the application of Kuyper's ideas to culture. There's a whole gaggle of guys out there attempting to locate art socially. When we get to the ideas of Francis Schaeffer and Hans Rookmaaker in England and America, that's good, and it's a darn site better than the way things were, because people on my end of things (the evangelical church of the time) had really cultivated a kind of insularity and nostalgia for the way things were and they turned it into a certain kind of place where you had to be if you were to call yourself a Christian.

I certainly benefitted from exposure to Schaeffer and Rookmaaker. It certainly set me on a path. I was seeing a lot of art and I was looking for some kind of approach to the arts that took into consideration the broader and swifter currents of what was going on. While I felt that Rookmaaker would be open to that conversation based on what I heard him say at the Royal College of Art, what you've got going on around and on the fringes, seemed to exhibit the same premature closure and apathy that one associated with other sections of the church at that time. That was my experience. There may have been a whole gaggle of people who were totally engaged and completely on track, relevant in their practice, I just didn't know about them.

GW: You once said, "How an idea is expressed has its own integrity and its own accountability." I almost feel that sums up the whole idea of your books.

SS: Yeah, someone else put it like this, talking about arts in the church. It's whether you communicate <u>with</u> art or <u>through</u> art. If you communicate with art,then art obviously has its own rules it's going to follow. If you communicate through art then whatever you do with the art is going to be subordinate to what you want to communicate. There's a prior rationalization that says, it's important that the message gets out or through, and you'll bend (artistic)rules for that purpose.

GW: So would you say with McLuhan that the medium is the message?

SS: To an extent, how you choose to communicate something will become part of what you communicate.

GW: At some point you were writing songs for the Scratch Band, which became the 77s.

SS: After I moved up from Los Angeles and began to get some music things going, Scratch Band came together. Sharon McCall was singing for them, with Mike Roe and Jan Eric Voltz and drummer, Mark Proctor (I think). They decided to cover one of my songs, "Different Kind of Light," which was going to be on Moving Pictures. They also did live versions of songs like "Wild Boys" and "The Thief Song" both of which were on a CD called 'Shirley, Goodness and Misery'.

GW: Why didn't Moving Pictures come out?

SS:. Things were getting increasingly foggy for me at Solid Rock Records: finish/ mix down and release dates kept getting pushed back. I finally gave up and left the project before it was finished.

All that to one side, regardless of the pros and cons of Solid Rock and or the stories that swirl around Larry Norman, I do think he's made an immensely valuable, foundational contribution to the whole contemporary Christian music industry…and I don't understand how someone that everyone nods towards and acknowledges as seminal ends up apparently scrabbling to pay for medical bills.

In my opinion, the ccm industry owes that guy so much for opening the door for so many people. If there was some kind of royalty structure attached to pioneering things and creating a huge market, you wouldn't think he'd be looking at any kind of financial worries.

GW: He's probably got post traumatic shock syndrome from being the visible target for anything and everyone from day one.

SS: The guy took all the bullets, created the market, and now (apparently) has to scrounge around to get money to stay alive. I'm not addressing the complex, legal, lawyer/ shark business aspect, I'm just saying that in real world terms (or `preferred real world'), he's owed a lot more than he's currently getting from those parts of the machine that benefited the most from his pioneering work.

GW: Do you see any recurring themes in your art?

SS: The constants are I like collage, I like juxtaposing things, in everything I was doing in film and poetry. I look for very simple rudimentary patterns and try and build around those patterns, whether it's a bass guitar sequence or film clips or the use of words.

GW: You're kind of minimalist in that respect.

SS: I wouldn't use the word 'minimalist," because my understanding of that concept/ label in art/ historical terms is the attempt to try and get back to the essence of the object or strip the relationship between the object and the viewer back down to its core constituents. Yes, I use very limited or minimal means, but for different reasons. I like kaleidoscopes and collage. I look for patterns when I'm writing poetry or writing songs or attempting some kind of visual thing, whether it be film or even in a book. If I write a full length book I will be looking for some sort of symmetry, resonance, emerging pattern. I'm more interested in things that start small but end up having multilayered effects. Like The Butterfly Effect, as my first spoken word album was called.

GW: Somehow you started making record albums.

SS: I started to write songs about local situations and people I knew or books I was reading. I'd layer a book title over the top of a situation I was aware of with a friend, or if I'd been travelling, I'd layer in bits of travel journal or fragments of that at one point. Like in the song, "Emotional Tourist" on the Lost Horizon CD, it has bits from Berlin, bits from being in a taxi cab in Delhi, India. They're all woven or stitched together.

The character in "Emotional Tourist" was probably the beginning of The Boundaries, which are poetry/ travel journals. That way of working was the beginning of the process for The Boundaries. Around the time that David Bowie's album, Lodger, came out, there was an interview in some rock magazine, New Musical Express or Melody Maker, and he was asked at one point because of all his exotic musical references whether or not he could be accused of just being an emotional tourist. And I thought, well that's an interesting turn of phrase! At that time also, I'd just seen Bowie in the film, Merry Christmas Mr. Lawrence, the film based on the Laurens Van der Post book. This is where the ritual suicide image came from in the third verse. So I was just stealing stuff from really good people, mashing it together, hanging it on a sort of improvised framework of things I was going through. Things from here and there, fragments of travel journal, bits from a film I'd just seen, so the song process and the song content was very much about skipping from surface to surface.

GW: But somehow having a visceral impact.

SS: I felt the song had a certain kind of impact. I felt it created a picture of someone who never gets beyond the surface of things. If my record, Love in the Western World set up certain kinds of personnae and knocked them down, talking very glibly about romantic love or the collapse of language or what have you, all the big ideas, in a very glib, self-referential, poppy kind of way, then "Emotional Tourist" went further and began to probe the idea of geography as history. In the song, "This Sad Music," I used a remote control to click between a TV preacher and a newscast on dying whales, and the extension or variation of that approach. At last, if we follow the line into 'Emotional Tourist' and some of the later spoken word stuff, we come up with a series of "wish you were here" postcards referencing other cultures. Although as my exposure to some of those cultures deepened, my work and ideas began to change.

Chronologically, Love in the Western World was the first album, released on the Exit label around 1983-'84. Moving Pictures was from the late '70s, and bits of it have leaked onto other projects. Then there was the Emotional Tourist album, which never came out as such, and turned into Lost Horizon. It was supposed to come out on Exit/ A&M, and at one point I think it was in the pipeline for Island Records. They did put out albums by the 77s and Charlie Peacock, who had both been on Exit. Magnificent Obsession came out with tracks that weren't on Lost Horizon plus some live stuff. (Lots of hats off and applause to Randy Layton and Alternative Records for stepping in and resurrecting those projects and putting his muscle and money and stuff into being Alternative Records to get that stuff out). After that I did a spoken word project for Mike Knott's record company, Blonde Vinyl Records, called The Butterfly Effect. And applause to Chris Rhumba for getting me to Blonde Vinyl!

GW: That is an amazing album. What you call spoken word many people would call performance art.

SS: Yes, that's like throwing the word "minimalism" around. Performance art, as I recall, was where people stepped away from the canvas on the wall and actually put themselves in real time: Joseph Beuys living in a room with a coyote for three days, Christopher Burden having himself nailed to a volkswagen. At the more accessible end of performance art would be someone like Laurie Anderson, who came out of a hard core gallery approach to things into a more populist, mixed-media approach.

GW: Do you morph at all into your other spoken word albums? Is there any change or is it continuing down the same path?

SS: It's definitely changing, but all the art I do revolves around rudimentary patterns and approaches to collage. The Butterfy Effect began by creating these sound loops in the studio and reading poems over the top. By the time we get to my later spoken word album, We Dreamed That We Were Strangers, the work that I'm doing in The Boundaries, which is a collection of travel journals and poems or poetic commentary on those travel journals, that's starting to shade into what I'm doing in the recording studio. I'm reading sections of The Boundaries over the top of sound loops, so the album begins to draw more on the prose and poetry of the emerging Boundaries sequence of books.

After that I did a project called Empty Orchestra. While I was in Holland touring The Butterfly Effect we started playing back the backing tracks. And we said, wouldn't it be great to put an album of real minimal, ambient loops out. So Empty Orchestra was that project, Empty Orchestra is the literal translation of 'karaoke'. So I wanted to do an album where everyone could be Steve Scott for a day so long as the only part of Steve Scott you want to be is the person doing spoken work performances. We printed the poems on the sleeve so that people who were sick of the sound of my voice could be me for the day.

I think More Than a Dream came next. That was a side step back to the rock songs. Empty Orchestra, We Dreamed That We Were Strangers, More Than a Dream and Crossing the Boundaries were all projects taken on by the late, lamented Mike Lucci. Mike and Heidi Lucci, then living in Kansas City, got involved in putting on local events and they had me come out to Kansas to do something like a lecture on the arts and a poetry reading. They started a local 'zine and they had me write some stuff for them. It was called Entire Vision. Mike got hooked up with Mike Delaney of Rad Rockers and brought my projects in under Rad Rockers. Mike Delaney, God bless him, stepped out and was no longer just a guy keeping a lot of really good alternative Christian music visible, but he also got into the business of putting out Steve Scott projects on Glow Records. Initially championed by the Lucci family, Delaney stepped in and put his shoulder to the wheel and he is and was Mr. Record Label.

All these guys: Larry Norman, Randy Layton, Randy Stonehill, the Luccis, Delaney. They're all due incredible amounts of adulation and applause and flowers and chocolates for what they did to basically keep Steve Scott artistically afloat. Along with Exit Records, and the Neelys and the Warehouse. All those things are very, very good and nothing would be happening without that, but I really think a lot of credit is due to the groupthought of Larry Norman, the enterpreneurial aspects of Randy Layton, the Luccis, Mike Delaney, and of course yourself: all guys on the cultural fringe who believe in something and just keep pushing to make it happen.

GW: I still think, like I wrote in The Gargoyle, which is the journal of the Malcolm Muggeridge Society in London, that you really ought to be on Virgin Records or some label like that.

SS: I'm ready when they are. Glow Records did put some albums out. There's one called 'More Than a Dream' which we can desribe as idiosyncratic.

GW: There's an excellent song on that album called 'Descending of the Dove', and does it or does it not remind me of Charles Williams' book, The Descent of the Dove?

SS: That's where I stole the title from. Someone wrote to me and said "We would be playing 'Descending of the Dove' in our church as a praise song, but for the out of tune singing in the chorus."

GW: That's of course the part I like.

SS: Yes, it's sort of like an Irish pub song, with me playing tin whistle.

GW: And how many churches have you been to where everyone's singing on key? Completely off the track, will there be any Steve Scott downloads?

SS: I don't know. What would be better is if bands wanted to do their own versions of my songs. I've got more book projects, one on the arts in progress called In the Shadow of God. It is a follow up to Like A House on fire and Crying for a Vision. What I really want to do is more spoken work projects. I have sound loops made from ambient recordings made in southeast asia and eastern europe. I've been combining these things and coming up with multilayered and multitextured sound beds, and I have the poems to read over the top. I need to finish the tracks and CDs and complete the cover designs and go. I also need to finish The Boundaries. About a third of it has been published in various volumes, but the new edition will be a one volume edition called The collected Boundaries.

15. Crying for a Vision Study Guide

The intent of this brief guide is to open up Steve Scott's Crying for a Vision for reflection and discussion. The questions follow along with each chapter, and can be used in a group setting, or with a journal for individual study and reflection. Many approaches are possible. A Bible study group can look up the various Scripture references in each chapter as a basis for discussion. An arts group can create individual or group projects that "incarnate" ideas in the readings. A reading group can read each chapter, using the guide questions to facilitate discussion. Any of these ideas can also be used for individual study. Further resources are listed in the Endnotes, and the reader is encouraged to take an individual and experimental approach to these questions in developing their own vision.

Chapter 1: Are You Responsible for This Monstrosity?

1. Steve Scott contrasts gift giving in a traditional society that is "spiritually bonded," and our society where a gift is a "free" commodity with "no strings attached." Discuss the difference between these views.

2. What is "autonomy?" Do we confuse "freedom" with "autonomy?" "Value" with "price?"

3. Scott gives three reasons for the practice and enjoyment of arts in the church.

How do the arts show (1). the creative aspects of our redeemed humanity?

How can they (2). build a bridge between cultures?

How do they (3). provide models for theological discussion?

Group project: Bring or make an artwork and show how it demonstrates one of these three areas.

Chapter 2: The Act of Seeing With One's Own Eyes

Scott provides four ways to look at art. Group project: Bring an artwork (your own or other's) What do you find by looking at it one or more of these ways?

Inside Looking Out.

4. Is this way of disinterested contemplation the way we usually look at art?
5. What effect does the museum system have on how we look at art?
6. Why does Suzi Gablik think that "pure" art is most easily co-opted by advertising, etc.?
7. Media critic Marshall McLuhan maintained that the artists of today are working for Madison Avenue (in advertising). Group project: bring examples of art in advertising for discussion. How does the art aid the advertisement? How is it "co-opted"? Are the messages in a 1950s ad different than the ones in a 200s ad?
8. If "modern" art is "pure" art in Gablik's sense, how is it "co-opted as "corporate" art? For example, how is a modern sculpture in a bank building different than the same sculpture in a museum? What does it say about the bank? About the museum?

Down Looking Up.

This way looks through art, not at it, to say something about the art in relation to society.

9. Consider the statement, "What the wealthy own is by definition good" in relation to art. What is the relation of wealthy art patrons to the museum system? Do they get their idea of what is good art from the museum? Or is the museum the result of their patronage of art?
10. How does modern art reflect these three views of society? Give examples.
    (1). Society is "in flight" from God (Schaeffer, Rook-maaker).
    (2). Loss of a shared symbolic order (Peter Fuller).
    (3). Art is divorced from the rest of life (Suzi Gablik).
11. "Anti-art declares the "end of art" in order to confront society. Give examples from dada(ism), punk rock or other "anti-art" movements.
12. In "anti-art," Scott says, the revolution is marketed as a commodity back to the masses (consumers). How does a punk rock album sell an illusion of "effective confrontation?" What are other examples of a revolution repackaged as a commodity?

Outside Looking In.

13. What does a frame mean around a picture? What "signals" does being in a museum give off about a particular sculpture or painting?
14. How does "disinterested contemplation" take place in a gallery? In what sense is the "disinterested" visitor involved?
15. How is contemplation of an art object in the West like/unlike quiet meditation in the East?

Change Consciousness/ Perception.

This is the attempt to use art for some other purpose: consciousness raising or to bring enlightenment. John Cage, in his performance of "Silence," sat down at the piano and did not play anything. The "performance" was about the formalities of preparing to play the piano and the expectation of the audience, who could then perhaps hear the "silence" as if it were music. Group project: Do a report to the group on John Cage.

16. A zen koan is a riddle designed to bring enlightenment: What is the sound of one hand clapping? There is also a zen practice of listening to your own breathing. Do you think that Cage's performance might help his audience listen to the silence?

17. A work of art is in some ways a "gestalt," a total unity that is more than the sum of its parts. In what sense can a work of art give us this sense of unity and harmony? In what sense can it awaken us to a larger sense of unity and harmony?

18. Chaos theory is a branch of science that explores the relationship between randomness and order. A Jackson Pollock canvas seems to be all randomness, while The Mona Lisa seems to be all order. Steve Scott named one of his albums The Butterfly Effect after the idea in chaos theory that something as small as the movement of a butterfly's wings can affect something as large as the weather system. Explore the relationship of randomness and order in an artwork.

19. Using fractal geometry, beautiful and intricate patterns called fractals can be generated on a computer from a simple equation which is iterated over and over. Group project: Get a shareware program to generate fractals or bring examples, as in Fractals for Windows (the Waite Group Publishing) or John Brigg's Fractals: The Patterns of Chaos.

20. Scott says, "Maybe we need, as artists, to stretch and play a little to shake off the years of 'spiritual' cobwebs, and break out of the straightjacket of sugar-coated pietism." Do you agree? Why or why not? What are some spiritual

cobwebs in your own life? What could you do to shake them off?

Group project: Make playful art in the group setting or individually and share it with the group. What straightjacket are you breaking out of? What cobwebs are you shaking off?

21. How might a "covenant partner" differ from a "co-creator" view of the artist? J.R.R. Tolkien talks about the artist as a "sub-creator," contrasting God, who creates out of nothing (ex nihilo), with the artist, who creates from materials that already exist ("Tree and Leaf" in The Tolkien Reader, Bantam Books). How might a "sub-creator" differ from a "co-creator"?

22. Scott cites artists widely separated in time as "a cloud of witnesses." Group project: Introduce one of these artists (or another artist) to the group. How could you view them as a "sub-creator" or "covenant partner?" Give examples from their work.

23. Find an artwork by this artist or another artist that does one of these three things:

   (1). "attacks accepted models of beauty and truth;"

   (2). "challenges the mythic status of the artist," or

   (3). "comes to terms with a plurality of cultures."

24. Scott discusses developmentally disabled persons as "marginalized" by society. How can art give marginalized persons "dignity and a dynamic symbol vocabulary?" What other groups are marginalized? Group project: Organize artmaking for a marginalized group.

25. Play with art to balance out the mental strain of reading this book.

Chapter Three: How Can You Use Something That Leaks?

26. Read John 5: 19 and 20. Jesus following the Father's example in healing someone, Scott says, is like a child watching a parent in a workshop. Read the story of the Korean craftsman. Pretend you are a child watching the craftsman. What do you learn?
27. Scott says that God's creative and redemptive acts are intimately related. Read Colossians 1: 15-22. What does Paul say about Christ's role in creation and redemption?
28. Scott discusses three levels of conflict.
    - (1). The clash between cultures, which relates to the role of the arts in that culture;
    - (2). The war within a culture, and how images and symbols are used at a popular level to wage such a war; and
    - (3). The war in the church and the heart and the conscience of the individual in relation to the culture and its worldview.

    Choose one of these levels. What barriers must the artmaker overcome? How can artmaking help bring peace to the conflict?
29. Scott says, "I believe that the church should seek to nurture the artist, and honor the symbol-making and image-bearing capacity of everyone, on one hand seeking to avoid hostility and misunderstanding, and on the other hand not succumbing to the temptation to glibly exploit

these capacities." How can the artist honor our symbol-
making and image-bearing capacity? What "exploits"
them?

30. "If art abandons a sign-hungry public," Scott says, "there
are plenty of other forces happy to move in to address that
deep-felt need for symbols and meaningful images, while
pushing an agenda of their own." What symbols and images in the church address our "sign-hunger?" What "other forces" might move in? What are their agendas? Group
project: Find examples in advertising that convey images
or symbols. What is their agenda? What is the relation of
the symbolism to the ad? Media critic Marshall McLuhan
said "The medium is the message," and "the medium is
the massage." How does the form of an advertisement
embody its message? (See The Medium is the Message"
and "War and Peace in the Global Village" by Marshall
McLuhan and Quentin Fiore, Bantam Books).

Chapter Four: Nothing More Than Dirt?

31. Read Genesis chapter two. What is the role of the Creator? The appreciator?
32. Consider the approaches of the biblical prophets Scott mentions as "art." Scott offers two challenges to artists:1.) skillful depiction of the seen and heard world; and 2.) an address to a prevailing human problem...or a particular cultural one." Group project: find or create art inspired by one of these two approaches. Consider these two approaches in relation to the roles of the Creator and appreciator.
33. How does Scott contrast the biblical prophets with punk rockers and anti-artists as "prophets?"
34. Scott asks "What works as a redemption story?" How could it be "outside?" How is it a "sign?"
35. Does it rob a story to explain its "spiritual meaning?" Why or why not?

Chapter Five: Freedom, Power and Creativity

36. What does Scott say here about God as Creator? What is the relation between creativity and limits?
37. Consider this quote from G.K. Chesterton: "All art is about limits; the most beautiful part of a painting is the frame." How does the medium limit a painting? How does the frame?
38. How does Scott relate art to Jesus' temptation in the wilderness? How does he view John chapter six?
39. Jesus risked what many artists shy away from, Scott says. "He engaged us both in terms of material and a particular cultural and historical reality. How did Jesus engage us in these ways? See also the essay, "The Dogma is the Drama" by Dorothy L. Sayers. This essay is available in various collections, including Letters to a Diminished Church, Creed or Chaos, and The Whimsical Christian.
40. How can art engage us in the ways Scott mentions above? Group project: create engaging art.

Chapter Six: Living Sacrifice/ Transformed Mind

41. What is "disembodied thinkng?" How can we "embody" thinking?
42. Listen to Steve Scott's song, "Flesh and Blood" (included on his CDs, Love in the Western World and Magnificent Obsession, available through RadRockers.com) or consider these lyrics from thc song:

He weren't no 3D hologram
he got up hungry and he went down tired
he felt the anger, he felt the sadness
he weren't a manequin that moved on wires
he never blinded us with party tricks
or strung us out on some astral fix
he weren't no voodoo child
or gentle Jesus meek and mild

He never told us that he was invincible
He didn't blind us with his x-ray eyes
He didn't come on like an extra terrestrial
hanging out in human disguise

flesh and blood, he wasn't no phantom
flesh and blood, he weren't no ghost.

(copyright Steve Scott, used by permission)

In Scott's song, who is Jesus? Who is he not? Group project: find a song that mentions Jesus. What kind of picture does the singer paint? If all you knew about Jesus came from the song, what sort of picture would you draw? Numerous songs offer varied pictures, from Leonard Cohen's "Suzanne" to Black Sabbath on Master of Reality. Larry Norman reviews some of these viewpoints in his song "Outlaw" from the album Only Visiting This Planet.

43. "Incarnation" means literally "in flesh" or "in meat" (Chili con carne is "chili with meat"). What is the relation of the Incarnation to "embodied thinking?"

44. Scott refers back to chapter one and the idea of exchanging gifts. Here he relates this idea to the gift of God's own Son. Read Ephesians 2: 6-10 and comment on Scott's statement, "we are set free, not merely to spin in anarchic, self-defeating circles, but free to creatively fulfill the purposes God equipped and designed us for before time."

45. Read the "upper Room" sequence in John chapters 13-17. If the gifts Scott refers to come through the gift of God's Son, what role can artists have in the community? What typifies the community's members?

46. Read Romans 12: 1-3. What does Paul mean by "present your bodies?" Make a list of attributes of being "in the body." What parallels can you draw with being in the Body of Christ? Thomas Howard says that "a body without a corpse; a spirit without a body is a ghost." (see Thomas Howard, Chance or the Dance, various editions from Harold Shaw publishers and Ignatius Press). What is special about the union of the body and spirit? Group project: make art that explores or celebrates being in the body (not a corpse or ghost).

47. How does the world (the electronic global village) attempt to duplicate the benefits of a relationship with God without God? (examples: cable TV, MTV, news, video games). Scott says this "world" tries to heal the sick situation through three false models of: 1). individuality; 2). community; 3.) history. Give examples of one of more of these false models. What would be a true model? Group

project: find examples of these false models in advertising, popular culture, etc. for group discussion. For a resource see Marshall McLuhan's War and Peace in the Global Village.

48. Scott talks about renewal through "crucified mind" thinking, which entails three things:

    1.) waking up to the mechanisms of control and reinforcement through art and media and in our own culture.

    2.) dying to notions of cultural superiority and appreciating diversity of cultural forms and expression.

    3.) coming alive to the imaginative, symbolic, narrative and artistic patterns available in the life of Jesus.

Comment on one of more of these three stages of renewal.

49. Does this renewal lead to this type of thinking or stem from it? Group project: express one of these types of renewal in your own art. Present it without comment. Let group members guess which of the three types of renewal it expresses and explore how it "embodies" that renewal.

Chapter Seven: Where Language Ends

50. Scott says, "The arts are able to serve us better...than some other forms of language." Comment on the Koestler quote. For a resource see Koestler's book The Act of Creation. Group project: introduce Koestler and his ideas to the group.

51. What kind of problems come from "above?" What kind from "below?" Creed comes from the latin word "credo," meaning "I believe." Read the Nicene, Athanasian or Apostles' Creed (the Roman Catholic creed is a version of the Nicene creed). How does the creed avoid the problems from above or below?

52. Discuss de Rougemont's idea of painting in relation to the earlier idea of creativity and limits. Scott here cites many artists and thinkers. See "Endnotes" to further explore their ideas.

53. Consider Judith Rock's idea of dance as a metaphor for the Incarnation.How can we think "with" and "through" art?

54. Consider another artistic medium (painting, sculpture, music, etc.). How can you think "with" and "through" it?

Chapter Eight: Towards a Lost Wax Mind

55. Read Hebrews 4: 12-15. What are the relations between an idea and an art object? Between form and content? Dorothy L. Sayers, in The Mind of the Maker, relates the process of creating to the three persons of the Godhead: Father, Son, and Holy Ghost. Group project: introduce Sayers and her ideas to the group.

56. Read Judith Rock's quote. What does Scott say about the relationship between an artwork and our response? How is this like or unlike that of a Creator and appreciator?

57. What are Scott's objections to making "really Christian art?" How can we show respect for our audience's humanity and God-given capacity for response?

58. Why would a culture that exhibits "the best of human creativity" be diverse in its expression? Group project: bring artwork from diverse cultures and comment on what you appreciate in each artwork.

59. Discuss "lost wax" thinking. If the wax image is taken to represent a "traditional spiritual impulse," what might be some of these impulses in the east, where the arts are "in place" in the culture? In the west, where the arts are "out of place" in the culture?

60. What three gifts does Scott say artists are given? Discuss one or more of these gifts. Group project: make art expressing one of these gifts.

16. Endnotes

PART ONE: CRYING FOR A VISION
CHAPTER ONE

[1] 'The Gift: Imagination and the Erotic Life of Property.'
Lewis Hyde.
Vintage Books/Random House 1983.

[2] A tremendous amount of research and practical work has been done on the use of art, ethnic arts and 'traditional media' in cross-cultural communication of the Christian message. I refer you to two excellent resources. FACE (Fellowship of Artists for Cultural Evangelism) directed by Gene and Mary Lou Totten. They have taught (on campus) classes and workshops on the subject, published a regular newsletter, and organized 'field trips' for 'working artists' groups onto American Indian reservations and beyond (way beyond...into Asia.) They can be contacted at 1605 East Elizabeth Street Pasadena, California 91104 USA.

Another good resource is Kathleen Nicholls, Traditional Media Unit coordinator for the International Christian Media Commission. She is based in India and regularly publishes a 'Traditional Media' newsletter with reports on developments from around the world. She (and her husband, Bruce) were also instrumental in organizing the 1989 Arts conference hosted by the Protestant Church of Bali. Her book 'Asian Art and Christian Hope' *(Select Books publishers and distributors 1983, New Delhi)* is an important resource. Kathleen D Nicholls E-56 Greater Kailash II New Delhi: 110048 INDIA.

[3] 'Crying for a Vision: Modern Art and the Christian Artist' *Radix Magazine March/ April 1982.*

CHAPTER TWO

[4] 'Art Beyond the MargIns' Suzi Gablik *New Art Examiner, December1989.*

[5] 'Ways of Seeing' John Berger, *BBC/Penguin Books 1972.*

[6] Jean Baudrillard, quoted by Maureen P. Sherlock in her essay 'Charades: a Critique of Corridor Criticism' included in ARTPAPERS *November/ December 1990.*

[7] See, for example 'Modern Art and the Death of a Culture' Hans Rookmaker *Downers Grove Ill.: Intervarsity 1970* and 'Escape from Reason' by Francis Schaeffer *Intervarsity 1968.*

[8] 'Images of God. The Consolations of a Lost Illusion.' Peter Fuller *Chatto and Windus 1985.* Fuller's books about art are all worth reading because of the valuable points he raised as he developed his body of ideas, beginning with 'Beyond the Crisis in Art' *Writers and Readers cooperative 1980.*

[9] See Suzi Gablik's 'Has Modernism failed?' *Thames and Hudson 1985,* also 'The Re-enchantment of Art' *1992.* Nicholas Wolterstorff's book is 'Art in Action.' *W.B. Eerdman's 1980.*

[10] See 'The Voices of Silence' Andre Malraux *Paladin 1974.*

[11]'The Aesthetic experience. An anthropologist looks at the vIsual arts' Jacques Maquet, *Yale University Press 1986.*

[12] Quoted by Calvin Tomkins in 'The Bride and the Bachelors: Five Masters of the Avant Garde' *Penguin Books 1976.*

[13] 'Rembrandt and the Gospel' W.A. Visser'T Hooft *Meridian Books 1960.*

[14] See these books for further reference.

'Art, Creativity and the Sacred' edited by Diane Apostolos-Cappadona. *Crossroad Books 1984.*

'A Theology of Artistic Sensibilities. The visual Arts and the Church.' John Dillenberger. *Crossroad Books 1986.*

'Style and Content in Christian Art.' Jane Dillenberger. *Crossroad Books 1988.*

[15] For more on this see 'Art in Action' by Nicholas Wolterstorff. *Publishing details above.*

[16] 'The Unknown Craftsman. A Japanese Insight into Beauty.' Soetsu Yanagi. *Kodansha International Ltd. 1972.*

[17] 'The Act of Creation' Arthur Koestler. *Macmillan 1964.*

[18] Ibid.

[19] Ibid

CHAPTER FOUR

[20] 'The Prophetic Imagination' Walter Brueggemann *Fortress Books 1978. See also:*

'Hopeful Imagination: Prophetic Voices in Exile'
Walter Brueggemann *Fortress books 1986*
'The Prophets, an Introduction' Abraham J. Hershel
Harper and Row 1962.

[21] 'Typology of Scripture' Patrick Fairbaim Originally published by *Funk and Wagnalls 1900.* Reprinted by *Kregel
Publications, 1989*

[22] 'Poet and Peasant: A Literary Cultural approach to the Parables In Luke' and 'Through Peasant Eyes' Kenneth Bai-
ley *Eerdmans 1976 and 1980* (4) Here are two examples.
There are more extensive examples provided throughout
the other chapters and their notes.

[23] 'Mark as Story. An introduction to the Narrative of a Gospel'
David Rhoads and Donald Michie *Fortress Press 1982*
'Anatomy of the Fourth Gospel. A Study In Literary
Design' R. Alan Culpepper *Fortress Press 1983*

[24] 'The Living Utterances of God: The New Testament Exege-
sis of the Old' Anthony Tyrrel Hanson *Darton, Longman
and Todd 1983*
'Biblical Interpretation in the Early Church' Karlfried
Froelich. *Fortress Press 1984*

[25] A Genre for the Gospels, the Biographical Character of
Matthew' Philip L. Schuler *Fortress Press 1982*

[26] 'Apocalyptic' Leon Morris, *Eerdmans 1972.*

CHAPTER SIX

[27] The major study on the 'cult of Romance' from a Christian point of view, is Denis De Rougemont's 'Love In the
Western World' reprinted *1983 Princeton University Press.*
Some of the implications of De Rougemont's study are
explored from a somewhat different, 'emerging paradigm'

perspective by Morris Berman in 'Coming to our Senses: Body and Spirit in the Hidden History of the West' *Simon and Schuster 1989.*

[28] 'The Act of Creation' Arthur Koestler *Macmillan 1964.*

[29] 'Yesterday and Today: A Study of Continuities in Christology' Colin E.Gunton *Darton Longman and Todd 1983*

[30] Koestler, *above*

[31] 'The Mission of the Artist' essay included in 'The Christian Opportunity' Denis De Rougemont, *Rinehart and Winston 1963*

[32] 'The Art of God Incarnate: Theology and Symbol from Genesis to the Twentieth century' Aidan Nicholls OP. *Darton, Longman and Todd 1980*

[33] 'The Theater of Revelation: Art and the Grace-fullness of Form.' Judith Rock *The Christian Century vol. lOS, no. 10*

[34] I intend this list to be useful and representative, rather than exhaustive. Consulting these volumes will give you guidelines for further exploration of the subjects.
    'The Eclipse of Biblical Narrative' Hans Frei *Yale University Press 1974*
    'Speaking in Parables, a study in Metaphor and Theology' Sallie MeFague *Fortress Press 1975*
    'The Great Code: The Bible and Literature' Northrop Fiye. New *York 1982* 'Theology and Narrative, A Critical Introduction' Michael Goldberg, *Abingdon 1982*
    'Story Shaped Christology: The Role of Narratives In Identifying Jesus Christ' Robert A. Krieg *CS.C. Paulist Press 1988*

'Why Narrative? Readings in Narrative Theology'
Edited by Hauerwas and Jones *Eerdmans 1989*
'Narrative Theology in Early Jewish Christianity' William Richard Stegner *Westminster/John Knox Press 1989*

[35] 'The Theater of God: Story in Christian Doctrines' Robert Paul Roth. *Fortress Press 1985.*

[36] Again, this list barely scratches the surface of the work being done. It's just a place to begin.

'Faith seeks Understanding' Arthur F. Holmes *Eerdmans 1971*

'Contours of a World view' Arthur F. *Holmes.Eerdmans 1983*

'Foolishness to the Greeks: The Gospel and Western Culture' Leslie Newbigin *Eerdmans 1986.* (An 'outside looking in' approach to 'post enlightenment culture as a missionary problem.')

'Towards a Post Critical Paradigm' James P. Martin. *New Testament Studies vol 13, 1987.* (Great overview of key trends with application to New Testament interpretation.)

'Symphonic Theology: the Validity of Multiple Perspectives in Theology' Vein. S. Poythress *Zondervan 1987*

CHAPTER EIGHT

[37] See Judith Rock, footnote 6, chapter 6.

About the Author

Steve Scott is a British-born poet, musician and performance artist whose songs have been recorded by artists including Larry Norman and the 77s. RadRockers.com called his CD, Love in the Western World, a "deliciously creepy, way-before-its-time alternative rock classic with similarities to David Bowie, Roxy Music and The Police...Lyrically deep and brilliant...an avant garde masterpiece with vocal inflections similar to Lou Reed." His other musical projects include The Butterfly Effect, More Than a Dream, Lost Horizon, Empty Orchestra, Magnificent Obsession, We Dreamed That We Were Strangers, and Crossing the Boundaries, in conjunction with painter Gaylen Stewart. He is the author of Like a House on Fire: Renewal of the Arts in a Postmodern Culture and The Boundaries. For more information please visit his official sites at canagroup.org and alivingdog.com.

Made in the USA
Lexington, KY
08 December 2010